THERAPY, INC.

A Hands-On Guide to Developing, Positioning, and Marketing Your Mental Health Practice in the 1990s

Linda L. Lawless

JOHN WILEY & SONS, INC.

New York • Chichester • Weinheim • Brisbane • Singapore • Toronto

This text is printed on acid-free paper.

Library of Congress Cataloging-in-Publication Data:

Lawless, Linda L.
Therapy, Inc. : a hands-on guide to developing, positioning, and marketing your mental health practice in the 1990s / by Linda L. Lawless.
p. cm.
Includes index.
ISBN 0-471-14760-5 (paper : alk. paper)
1. Psychotherapy—Practice—United States. 2. Psychotherapy—United States—Marketing. 3. Mental health services—United States—Marketing. I. Title.
RC465.6.L38 1997
616.89′14′068—dc20 96-35437

Printed in the United States of America

10 9 8 7 6 5

To all the mental health professionals who are struggling to stay active in their field, in the face of a changing and sometimes unfriendly marketplace. I hope the information in this book will motivate and empower you to develop your entrepreneurial strengths. May you reach your own definition of success as a professional businessperson, and may your success facilitate the use of your hard-earned professional skills.

ACKNOWLEDGMENTS

Like most long-term endeavors, this book wouldn't have been possible without the faith and support of colleagues and friends. A special thanks for the daily *just do it* from my husband Glen and the focus provided by my editor Kelly Franklin.

CONTENTS

QUICK REFERENCE GUIDE TO EXERCISES, WORKSHEETS, AND SAMPLES

1

INTRODUCTION

With the inception of behavioral healthcare in 1982, the old Chinese curse, *May you live during interesting times,* came upon us. To maintain a port in this storm of interesting times, many have tried to work harder at what they know best only to discover the work they love is slipping through their fingers. Seasoned professionals have found the old ways of creating a lifetime professional practice no longer work.

Although professional survival in the mental health field has certainly become more difficult in the past five years, mental health is still a relatively new field where change is the norm. To deal with these dynamic transformations, many practitioners have sought the shelter of stable positions in agencies and hospitals. Now, even those safe career moves are being eliminated as institutions struggle to survive despite buyouts and mergers. Today, more than ever, clinicians are uncertain how to secure their professional future. In this book I propose that rather than becoming the victims of change, we reframe our position as creators of solutions.

When looking for those solutions, practitioners must consider many variables. A holistic picture of the issues and trends must include answers to the following questions:

- What is the professional identity of the individual practitioner and what position are they taking in the larger mental health arena?
- What changes have occurred in:
  Clinical treatment methodologies?
  Behavioral healthcare?
  The private pay marketplace?
  Corporate America?
  Legislative actions?
  The medical field?
- What is the impact of alternative healthcare?
- What regional developments have taken place that affect the mental health field?

Start now to stay informed and ready to respond effectively to change. Before you read the rest of the book, subscribe to a few of the national periodicals in the mental health arena. Here are a few I have found to be valuable resources (I have included telephone numbers for your convenience):

- *OpenMinds* (1-717-334-1329).
- *The Family Therapy Networker* (1-202-829-2452).
- *Psychotherapy Finances* (1-407-747-1960).
- *Managed Care Strategies* (1-800-869-8450).
- *Practice Management Monthly* (1-800-578-5013).

In addition, *The Standard Periodical Directory* (available at your local library) lists periodicals in your areas of interest. Many publishers will send you a free preview issue of their publication. Simply call or write a request on your business stationery. Those of you who have not yet joined your national and regional professional associations should do so without delay; these organizations are a valuable source of information. If you have access to the Internet, browse the mental health sites for news. If you follow these recommendations and carefully read the materials you collect, you will be much better prepared to deal with the coming changes in the field.

You need more than information to create a successful professional practice. The materials in this book come from my 20-plus years of experience creating various types of successful business entities. When setting up a not-for-profit corporation, community group practice, individual practice, and group without walls, I needed information and guidance on how to proceed. Some areas of special importance for me were business start-up, marketing, public relations, business management, and the requirements for working with behavioral healthcare. I read many books designed for general business applications and some intended specifically for therapists. Most of these books were written by experts in their field (e.g., marketing, public relations). Because this material often did not speak to the unique experience of the professional mental health counselor, I had to translate the ideas to fit into my unique world of dual relationships, professional ethics, licensing, and legislative constraints. This book includes the translations as I see them.

The following chapters are designed to meet the needs of the first-time or potential private practitioner as well as the seasoned therapist in an individual setting or a group practice. The organizational structure proceeds from the start-up phase of practice development through the marketing and promotions necessary to develop your business.

Chapter 2, "Taking Stock of Where You Stand," helps you evaluate your individual situation or the starting point for your professional journey.

In Chapter 3, "Establishing a Practice," you will identify what you need in your professional-business bag for a successful future in the marketplace.

Chapter 4, "Analyzing Your Services," provides the marketing tools and information to move you toward your personal definition of success.

The concepts in Chapter 5, "Developing a Marketing Plan," revolve around issues we all face as self-promoters. Most mental health professionals find this task unsavory. I have reframed this task to make marketing something you do naturally and easily. You might even enjoy it.

The purpose of Chapter 6, "Making the Most of Your Marketing Tools," is to provide you with marketing tools you can comfortably use to promote your business.

Chapter 7, "Getting the Word Out: Publicity and Promotion," helps you understand self-promotion and use publicity and business promotion in a positive way.

The focus of Chapter 8, "Managing to Care," is on the current industrialization of the mental health profession. You will gain an honest and ethical perspective that will enable you to tool up and thrive in the behavioral health-care marketplace.

The final chapter is entitled "Change, Innovation, and Maintenance of Success." When you use the tools in the previous chapters, you will be creating change in your life. If you understand the change process and learn to operate effectively within change, you will stay dynamic and balanced. Innovation and creativity are explored as survival and optimal performance tools in our rapidly evolving profession.

If you have thought about leaving the field of mental health, I hope this book inspires you to reconsider.

2

TAKING STOCK OF WHERE YOU STAND

Professional Developmental Stages

The mental health professional passes through stages of development much like a child's phases of growth on the way to adulthood (Skovholt & Ronnestad, 1992). Just as you would not ask a child of two to train for a marathon, you would not ask a clinician with limited experience to supervise trainees. Identifying your stage of development will help you determine goals for developing your practice along with appropriate marketing strategies. For example, those who have reached the *Transition Stage* in their development usually find it easy to reframe their work and move into new arenas. Professionals in mid-course or *Conditional Autonomy* are less inclined to change their professional identity. It makes sense for them to explore new referral sources in their current arena. To explain these dynamics, Figure 2.1 summarizes the stages as identified by Skovholt and Ronnestad in their book *The Evolving Professional Self—Stages and Themes in Therapist and Counselor Development.*

Review these stages and ask yourself where you are today. You may see yourself in more than one category, as is often the case with any developmental process. We can be ahead one day and find ourselves backpedaling on another depending on circumstance and inner orientation.

Relating the Stages to Career Development

Each stage supports certain kinds of practice development. The idea is to operate out of the stage you primarily reside in. When you do this, you feel the most secure and authentic, and are more likely to act on your professional goals. The phases of professional and career development are defined in Figure 2.2.

Throughout all these stages, the professional will be working in a variety of settings. It is particularly important to know the optimal setting for your own professional development. Using this information in your marketing efforts is discussed in Chapter 5. The most fundamental

Figure 2.1

Stages in a Therapist's Development

Conventional Life Experiences

These individuals use conventional life experiences and common sense to solve problems. They often believe that love and understanding are the cure-alls for most problems. They are minimally aware of their motivations to enter the field but find they are drawn to it or have a calling.

Transition to Professional

Students enter training and begin to integrate their new learning and training experiences into their previous strategies. They gain insight into their reasons for entering the field and invest much time and personal energy seeking a methodology that makes sense to them. They find many similarities in the models they explore and see them reflected in their own life experiences and family dynamics.

Imitation of Experts

There is an attempt to internalize attitudes and behaviors of expert models with which the new practitioners find an affinity. A range of approaches is possible in this stage. Some align with a single model and others become eclectic or use an intuitive approach. As these professionals gain more experience and begin to feel a level of expertise, they may either explore their own issues in more depth or close the door to personal exploration.

Conditional Autonomy

Professionals experience more socialization and enculturization in their field. They acquire a variable sense of competence based on internal and external standards about performance. They are in the process of understanding client dynamics and the change process that takes place in therapy. If they are exploring their own issues, they develop an inner observer that watches them as they relate and work with others.

Exploration

According to Skovholt and Ronnestad (1992), this stage involves "Exploration for self by self with self as director." Professional confidence and alternating anxiety dominate their

(Continued)

Figure 2.1 *(Continued)*

affective experiences. There is an awareness of the complexity of the profession with increased recognition of the importance of the therapeutic relationship. They gain greater clarity of their role with clients and perceive how, what, and why change does or does not take place. The learning process is through reflection and objective observation of the self at work.

Integration

The dominant task here is the development of professional authenticity. The primary affect is satisfaction with one's work. There is a greater willingness to acknowledge how one's personal life affects work. The working style of these practitioners is less rigid with more flexibility. Their unique personalities, all that helped create them, emerge into their work. At this point, peer supervision is a rich field for learning and exploration of theories.

Individuation

The deepening authenticity in the practitioner's work evolves and is supported by a vision of the future. The challenge here is to develop a consistent style while still growing and learning rather than stagnating and burning out through intellectual apathy and emotional exhaustion. There is an increased ability to use the self as an instrument and to empathize and be present with the client. Paradoxically, these clinicians can distance from client involvement when not working. Learning now takes place in a self-directed mode that draws from educational and life experiences. There is less need for external praise and validation.

Integrity

The professional may contemplate transitioning out of the field or preparing for retirement. The dominant affect is acceptance. There is a greater ability to take risks in treatment and learn from client responses. Accumulated knowledge and experience from a broad range of fields in the humanities is the central source of influence. Personal satisfaction comes from a deep understanding of what the work involves, including a balanced life.

Transition

The practitioner begins the process of retiring or changing professional identities and integrating them with the personal and private sense of self.

Figure 2.2

Phases of Career Development

The Explorer (Conventional Life Experiences)

There is a "sense of a quest" in this beginning stage of future mental health professionals. They have not yet been formally trained but may explore their desire to enter the field through volunteer or entry level work.

The Student (Transition to Professional)

This is where formal training takes place. The student is usually strongly shaped by educational settings and internships. These experiences allow the mental health professional to explore their educational choices in the field carefully before choosing a school or internship location.

The Practice Begins (Imitation of Experts)

Every professional remembers their first client and how it felt to be in this new role of "healer." Often there is some feeling of being an impostor. This is a good time for practitioners to declare a specialty based on the treatment methodology they are the most expert in. Examples of well-known techniques are group therapy, gestalt therapy, behavior management, cognitive restructuring, and family therapy.

Reaching Out (Conditional Autonomy)

This stage fosters a desire to reach out to other practitioners and talk about clinical approaches. If marketing tools are in place they can be distributed with great confidence. Marketing materials from the previous stages can be used, especially if the professional maintains a thread of continuity from one stage to another.

Reframing the Work (Exploration)

The professional relationships that have developed can now be used to dialogue about new ideas concerning the work. Networking is a natural marketing tool. This can be a creative time of group brainstorming in search of new applications of old knowledge.

(Continued)

Figure 2.2 *(Continued)*

The Promotion of Work through Self (Integration)

At this point it becomes easier for professionals to market themselves. They may create a personal brochure. Now is a good time to invest in a logo or graphic design if it has not already been done.

Sharing Insights (Individuation)

There can now be a further development of the identity of the professional as the primary professional resource. Many practitioners find it is a good time to write about their insights into their work. Relationships with colleagues may become more hierarchical with others wanting to model after or learn these new approaches.

Diversification (Integrity)

The unique insights gained from years of experience can now be translated and applied to other professional areas such as teaching, training, or consultation. The professional though, still identifies himself as a mental health professional.

Moving On (Transition)

At this stage, psychotherapists can easily change their identity to that of consultant, trainer, motivational speaker, or other professional or business identity. They may or may not choose to remain an "expert" in the mental health field.

variable is your preferred relationship to others while you work.

WORK RELATIONSHIP STYLE

Just as plants and animals prefer certain environments, people flourish in compatible relationships. It is helpful to identify the environment in which you work best. The "Work Relationship Style" worksheet shown in Figure 2.3 will help you identify your preferred working environment. You may get a more accurate score if you complete the worksheet before you read on.

The section of the Work Relationship Style worksheet with the highest score reflects your primary current preference. The following descriptions will clarify and suggest your optimal work environment.

The Partnership

If this profile produced your highest score and your present occupation requires that you work with a team, you may be in a less-than-ideal working environment. Other clues that might indicate your partnership personality are:

- You usually have had one close friend, even as a child.
- You married early.
- You share easily with a trusted individual.
- You are happiest when paired, in romance, in sports, at dinner, and so on.
- You are fascinated with duos of any kind, in love, work, or play.
- Famous teams intrigue you, and you'd like to be part of one yourself.

Remember, these are simply clues—not fixed rules.

A successful partnership involves not only a willingness but a strong desire to include the other. You perform at your best when creating together. A partnership will work only if both individuals are mature, self-confident, and happy to see the other become successful. A rare and beautiful relationship can develop if you're a partner type and can find the right working partner.

Team Relationship

The person who flourishes in the team environment is a specialist at whatever he or she does. This individual enjoys the camaraderie of the larger group where decision making is spread around. Plenty of discussion, consensus agreement, and the group's benefit are all highly regarded. The team works for each member who is willing to play his or her part and play it well. Team players enjoy the rivalry between and among other departments, companies, and fields valuing their team within the larger framework. As a team type, you wilt without comrades to share your defeats and victories. Loneliness is your biggest fear. Other clues to the team player:

- You came from a large family.
- As a child, you played with a group of friends.
- You had early positive experiences with large families.
- You can maintain several relationships at once, lovers, friends, and so on.

The team player thrives in cooperative, competitive stimulating environments. You are a lusty, hardy, cheerful participant when you are on a compatible team.

Figure 2.3

Work Relationship Style

Circle the number to any of the following statements that apply to you. Skip the statements that do not apply.

1. I enjoy give-and-take ideas in conversation and decision making.
2. I have a few long-lasting intimate friendships.
3. I find that my creativity increases when I work with another person.
4. I consider myself to be self-reliant.
5. I enjoy listening to other people's ideas and concepts.
6. I prefer to pool resources, money, ideas, property, knowledge. I feel more powerful with shared riches.
7. I see a partnership as a shared independence between equals.
8. I do not do well with authoritarian relationships.
9. I enjoy the feedback and encouragement from someone I work closely with.
10. I prefer to share risk taking with one other person.
11. I love competition and rivalry as a motivator.
12. I form many friendships easily.
13. I believe I am gregarious and outgoing.
14. I am comfortable with authority figures who are competent, and I respond well to a good leader.
15. I find that my creativity increases with abundant praise from my teammates and our leader.
16. I see relationships as cooperative units within a larger structure.
17. I am loyal and conscientious.
18. I belong to clubs, groups, and organizations. I enjoy the society of others.
19. I enjoy working with groups of people.
20. I like to be alone about 20 percent of the time. Most of the time I prefer companionship.

(Continued)

Figure 2.3 *(Continued)*

21. I am resourceful and self-contained, and I like my privacy.
22. I find that my creativity increases with freedom. I believe I have an inventive, imaginative, artistic, contemplative mind.
23. I am an independent risk taker.
24. I choose my friendships carefully and prefer others who are independent.
25. I strongly resist authority. The more autonomy I have the better.
26. I prefer to work alone. I need time to ruminate ideas on my own.
27. I believe the act of creation itself is the most important stimulant for further creativity.
28. I enjoy praise from my accomplishments.
29. When I work on a project by myself, time passes quickly.
30. I prefer to have my own work setting rather than share a space.

Total the number of statements circled in sections:

1–10 ____________ Partnership Score

11–20 ____________ Team Score

20–30 ____________ Going Solo Score

Going Solo

Are you happiest when you are in charge? Do you like to make all the decisions? The solo type likes to say, *I did that.* "That" can be the business he or she builds, the sale made, or the book written. The key to this personality is the desire to wear all the hats. The solo strongly resists outside influence and does not feel comfortable on teams or in partnerships unless personal autonomy can be maintained.

The preceding description suggests that the solo type will be miserable in a large, highly structured company or organization (except as the president). If you're a solo, you like to make up the rules as you go. Other clues:

- As a child, you were extremely imaginative and daydreamed a great deal.
- You had imaginary playmates.
- You imagined being on stage alone as a performer.
- You had early experience with entrepreneurship.
- You made your own money early.
- You are drawn to individual sports.
- The individual star fascinates you.
- You have great powers of concentration.
- You love nature—being alone in the woods is your idea of heaven.

In an environment that respects their independence and potential for leadership, solos can have a lasting, beneficial impact on society.

These three types, partnerships, team, and solo are not mutually exclusive. For example, a solo can work within a partnership if the other individual is similarly iconoclastic and freedom-loving. Such a pair of individuals would not exert control or restriction on each other.

It is not uncommon to be a combination of types, but usually one type exerts greater influence. Being aware of this trait will help you more accurately define your goals and your passion. It is rewarding and useful to discover your work relationship style. This knowledge is essential in finding the optimal working situation. With this information, you can shape your working relations, no matter what circumstances you encounter. If you work better alone and find yourself part of a group, try to carve out a particular job for yourself that reports to the group. If you work best in partnership, find a person you believe you will work well with and choose a task the two of you can complete and then take back to the group. On the other hand, if you work best with a partner or in a group but find yourself alone on a project, begin networking to create your own group or find another group you can work with.

Choosing Specialties

You will find it advantageous to declare specialty areas. If you market yourself as an expert in one or more areas, people will think of you when they identify those areas of need and you will receive referrals. You must have formal training and experience in any specialty area you declare to protect yourself from potentail malpractice claims. Many managed care companies require that specialty providers have documented training. Don't specialize in too many areas; trying to be all things to all people will reduce your credibility.

Start with your present practice when you choose your specialties. Ask yourself, *What arenas do I work well in and enjoy?* If you already have specialties, ask yourself why you chose them and whether they accurately reflect

Figure 2.4

Choosing Specialties

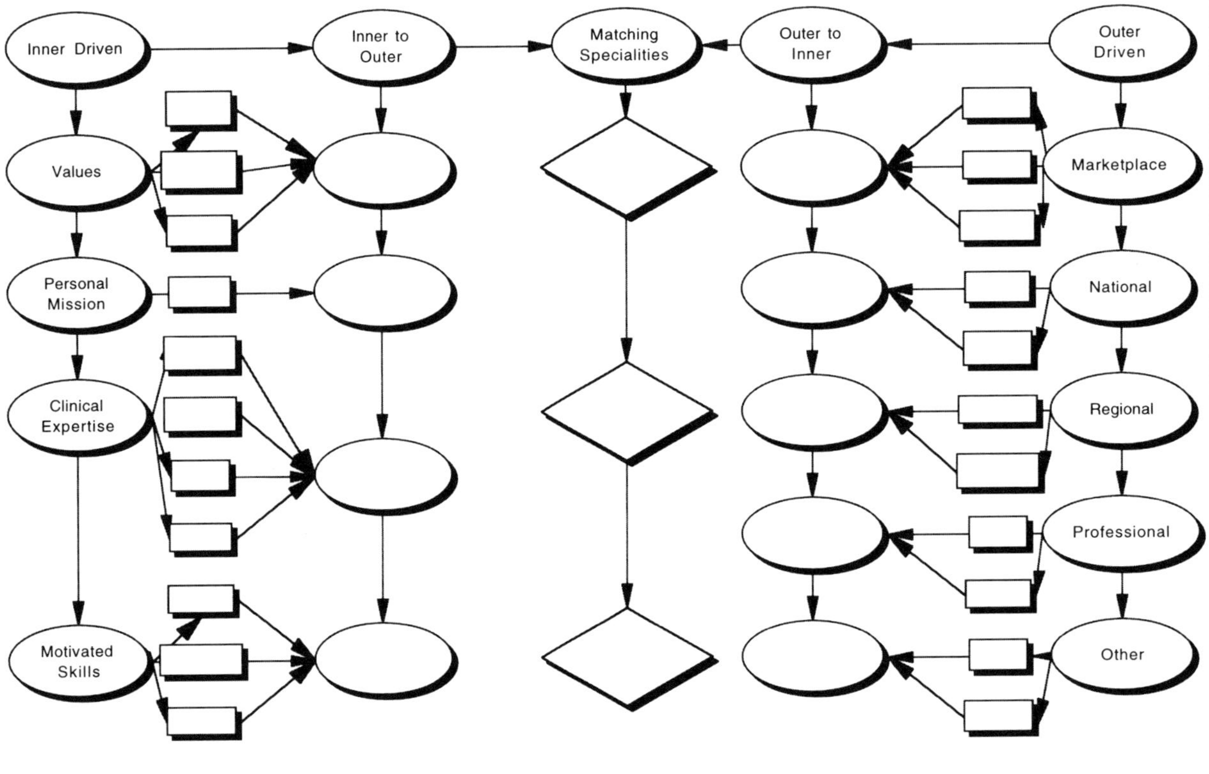

your expertise as a therapist. Look inward and find those skills; then look outward and identify the needs you see in the community. Is there a match? If not, look outward toward the marketplace and identify the areas that are currently being recruited. Now look at your skills and ask yourself, *Can I ethically offer services in any of these arenas?* You may able to provide what is called a *carve-out* service in one of the current arenas. For example, in the area of eating disorders, you may already have training in addictions but do not have experience with food addictions. The overlap might allow you to offer services in the area of your expertise while you receive further training or supervision to expand into the new specialty area. The diagrammed worksheet shown in Figure 2.4 will help you find a match between your skills and what is being recruited in the marketplace. Do not fall into the trap of being market driven. If you choose a specialty simply to make more money, it might be a good short-term solution for your finances but not a long-term success for your career. Use the following process to fill in the worksheet:

1. Start with the left-hand column (Inner Driven) and fill in your primary values, work goals, clinical expertise, and other motivated skills.
2. In the right-hand column (Outer Driven), fill in the jobs and skills that are being driven by national agendas, regional needs, professional trends, or any other dynamics in the marketplace.
3. Now develop the "Inner to Outer" and "Outer to Inner" columns. Look at the "Inner Driven" information and compare it with the "Outer Driven" information. Look for matches as well as areas you could reframe or move into with a little more training or experience. You might also consider partnering with people whose skills complement yours.
4. In the center column, identify at least three services or products that use your inner-driven specialties and are valued in the marketplace.

These are the specialties to be used in your primary market promotions. An approach to singling out choosing specialties is outlined by Anthony Putman in his book *Marketing Your Services* (Putman, 1990). Complete Figure 2.5 to identify the best business vehicle to move you toward professional success.

Now that you have identified your professional specialties, you need to describe the benefits for your clients. This is another step in defining yourself in the mental health marketplace.

PROFESSIONAL PROFILE

Creating a professional profile clarifies your personal identity as a professional. These documents are often requested by potential managed care provider panels and agencies, and can be used with media releases. You probably already have a curriculum vitae or resume but you should also create a Professional Biography, a Professional Narrative, and a Practice Information Summary. One of the most valuable benefits of creating these descriptions is that you must look objectively at yourself and your professional services. This often proves to be one of the most difficult tasks for therapists who are learning to market themselves.

Professional Biography

The Professional Biography briefly describes your training and experience and lists the services that you currently offer. Use this biography under your picture in media releases or on your brochure. It should be tailored for the audience that will be reading it. Emphasize different information depending on the values of the target audience. I find it helpful to have a long version and a short version that I can quickly modify when necessary. Figure 2.6 shows a sample thumbnail biography; Figure 2.7, a medium-length biography; and Figure 2.8, a long version for organizations that want more detailed information about this provider.

Follow the steps outlined in Figure 2.9 to create your own biographies. Start with a short form and work toward a detailed or long version.

You will need a good black and white professional photograph of yourself for promotional purposes. Copies should be made in two sizes, 5×7 inches and $8\,½ \times 11$ inches.

Figure 2.5

Niche Market or Ideal Client

What phrase or term identifies members of this niche market?

1.

2.

3.

Rating Your Ideal Clients			
Rate each one from 1–10 1=low/10=high	1	2	3
1. This niche market has money			
2. This niche market will pay a premium for good service			
3. There is a large population in this market			
4. Competition in this area is low			
5. I can easily get my information to the decision makers			
6. I already have credibility with this niche market			
7. The members of this market have a high perceived need			
8. This market already knows they need what I offer			
9. This niche market is in the right geographic area			
TOTAL SCORE			

(Continued)

Figure 2.5 *(Continued)*

Rate each niche market in every category from 1 to 9 and total them at the bottom. The niche market with the highest total score is the one with the highest potential for marketing success.

Using the Ideal Client that scored highest ask yourself the following questions:

What kind of information impresses this population?

What personal experience do I have with this population?

What important need(s) do I meet for this marketplace?

What kinds of services already exist to fill the need(s)?

Who actually makes the decision to purchase services or products?

How can I best reach the decision maker?

Figure 2.6

Thumbnail Biography

Susan Froid, LMFT, LMHC, has been in the field of mental health for over 20 years. As owner of Therapy Inc., Ms. Froid provides practice consultation, professional career development, and offers counseling services for managed care and individuals. Her clinical specialty is eating disorders. Ms. Froid travels nationally to lecture and train professionals in designing, managing, and developing their professional practices and careers. (63 words)

Figure 2.7

Medium-Length Biography

Susan Froid, LMFT, LMHC, has practiced in the field of mental health for over 20 years. After working in the aerospace industry as a methods analyst, she trained and worked in the California state mental hospital system for 15 years. Her experience in that setting ranged from psychiatric nursing to managing a 40-bed residential unit and leading a treatment staff of over 40 professionals. After graduating with a Master's Degree in Clinical Psychology and receiving her license as an MFCC (Marriage, Family, Child Counselor), Ms. Froid left state service and cofounded a nonprofit counseling group *Gateway Counseling.* She later cocreated a successful community counseling resource *Benicia Counseling Center.* Politically, she sat on the Solano County Mental Health Advisory Committee Board, which provided recommendations to the county supervisors on how best to appropriate funds for the mental health needs of the county. She wrote a community service directory *People Helping People* to help individuals more easily access human services. She also consulted with small businesses mediating management problems and creating strategic growth plans.

Since relocating to Massachusetts four years ago, Ms. Froid has cofounded a group without walls, the *Metro-Boston Professional Counseling Association.* She is also a cofounder of the *Professional Training Institute,* which offers training and consultation for the life span of the psychotherapist. As owner of Therapy Inc., Ms. Froid provides practice consultation and professional career development, and offers counseling and prevention programs to Managed Care and individuals. Her clinical specialty is eating disorders. She travels nationally to lecture and train professionals in designing, managing, and developing their own professional practices and careers.

Ms. Froid believes in the power of collaboration and encourages professionals to work with one another to create change. To her peers, she brings a hopeful vision of the future, and the inspiration to make it happen. (301 words)

Figure 2.8

Detailed Biography

Susan Froid, LMFT, LMHC, has been in the field of mental health for over 20 years. She entered it after working many years in management systems in the aerospace industry. For the first 15 years, she trained and worked in California State mental health hospitals and worked her way up the system from a nursing trainee to the position of Unit Charge. As Unit Charge, she had 24-hour responsibility for a 40-bed residential unit with a staff of over 40 professionals. She watched the effects of privatization during Reagan's tenure as governor of California and had direct experience with the stress-induced illnesses of inadequate staffing. She also knew there must be a better way to integrate clients into the community and support treatment staff in the process. After graduating with her Master's Degree in Clinical Psychology from J. F. Kennedy University in California and receiving her license as an MFCC (Marriage, Family, Child Counselor), she left state service and worked with a group of peers to start a nonprofit counseling group *Gateway Counseling.* Being a single parent, she decided to bring her work closer to home. To this end, she collaborated with two colleagues to create the *Benicia Counseling Center,* a successful community counseling resource. While in California, she was involved at a local level on the Solano County Mental Health Advisory Committee, which provided recommendations to the county supervisors on how best to appropriate funds for the mental health needs of the county. She coauthored a community service directory *People Helping People* that enabled community members to easily access human services.

Since moving to Massachusetts four years ago, Ms. Froid has cofounded a group without walls, the *Metro-Boston Professional Counseling Association—Independent Practitioners;* cofounded the Professional Training Institute, which provides training and consultation for the life span of the psychotherapist; and provides counseling and practice consultation through Therapy Inc. Ms. Froid's clinical specialty is eating disorders. She uses a holistic approach in her work, addressing the mental, emotional, physical, relational, and spiritual needs of her clients. She travels nationally to lecture and train other professionals how to collaborate with managed care as well as design and develop their own professional practices.

Ms. Froid's mission is to find a way to create a mental health delivery system that is as healthy for its users as it is for its providers. After moving to Massachusetts, she discovered how regionally specific the mental health delivery systems are and how

(Continued)

Figure 2.8 *(Continued)*

diverse the practitioner's experience is. Ms. Froid got involved with her professional organization at a national level and confirmed her suspicion that all clinician's need basic skills to define their own situation, its inherent problems, and the resources for change. Then, they need useful tools so they can prosper and create change. She also believes in the power of collaboration and encourages professionals to work with one another. To encourage optimism for the future, Ms. Froid has written many articles for professional magazines and newsletters and writes and self-publishes her own training manuals. To her peers, she brings a hopeful vision of the future and the inspiration to make it happen. (524 words)

Figure 2.9

Steps for Developing a Professional Biography

1. Identify your target audience. Who will be reading this biography? Adapt your basic biography for each audience. You will be emphasizing different information for the needs of your target audience.

Target audience: ______________________________

Short Biography

List the following information:

- Name.
- Current position.
- Past education including continuing education that applies to any declared specialties.
- Work experience.
- Present position and responsibilities.
- Past positions(s) and responsibilities.

2. Take the preceding information and write your short biography in paragraph form.

Detailed Biography

List the following:

- Professional goals.
- Areas of special interest and expertise.
- Other related professional affiliations.
- How you evolved into particular work efforts.

3. Take the additional information and write your detailed biography in paragraph form.

Professional Narrative

This narrative is different from the biography. The biography focused primarily on your work experience. The narrative describes your internships, training, and background as a professional. It includes your personal motivations to enter the field.

The first time a managed care company asked me for a professional narrative, I was at a loss about what to send and frantically called my colleagues for samples of theirs. Over the years, I have identified my professional narrative as a history or biography of my professional work. In your narrative, include the following information:

Who You Are

- Name.
- Licenses and certifications.
- Name of business.
- How long in business.
- How you arrived at what you do today.

Education and Training

- Training in areas of specialization.
- Ongoing continuing education.

Professional Experience

- Experience in areas of specialization.
- Ongoing training and supervision.

Overall, show how you have developed into the clinician you are today. Try to be as market-specific as possible with your information. I always ask myself, *What do these people want to read that I can provide honestly and ethically?* Your layout should allow the reader to look at blocks of information with the most important features in the first two or three sentences. Include more details in the rest of the paragraph. If you have a word processor, you might put the most important information in boldface type. Figure 2.10 shows a sample professional narrative.

In addition to a general narrative, you may want to prepare a separate narrative that focuses on your specialty. Figure 2.11 provides a sample specialty narrative.

Current Practice Information

This description of your present professional practice provides information that any potential client or referral resource needs to know before contracting for your services. Your practice information will change as your practice expands and evolves. Keep your information current by reviewing it quarterly and sending updates to any companies for which you provide services. Your *Practice Information* sheet should include:

Who You Are

- Your professional name.
- Name of business.
- Length of time in business.

Services

- Areas of specialization (supported by Professional Narrative and curriculum vitae).
- Benefits of your services. Include three for each specialty. Figure 2.12 shows two sample benefits statements for treatment modalities.

Figure 2.10

Sample Professional Narrative

Susan Froid, LMFT, LMHC
Professional Narrative and History

Education and Training

I have worked in the field of mental health since 1971 and have been in private practice since 1983. My formal training began in the field as a Psychiatric Nurse Intern at Fairview State Hospital in California. I progressed into management as a Senior Psychiatric Technician II (24-hour charge of a residential unit) while I continued my education. I graduated with a Master's Degree in Clinical Psychology in 1985.

After leaving the hospital, I expanded my clinical work to a community-based counseling center directed by J. F. Kennedy University (JFK). At JFK, I counseled individuals, couples, families, and children. My clinical work was guided by a teaching team that observed counseling sessions through a one-way mirror. Once each week, a critique of my work came from my professors and experts in the field. I was licensed in 1985 as a Marriage Family and Child Counselor (MFCC) in California. I cofounded a community-based group counseling practice that year, and in 1987 I began training MFCC interns at the center. Clinical case seminars were ongoing at our center.

In 1990, I relocated to Massachusetts and completed licensure in 1991 as a Marriage Family Therapist and a Mental Health Counselor. I conducted professional training seminars for mental health professionals to help counselors prepare for and complete licensure, then design and develop a practice. I regularly attend five to seven professional development classes each year to upgrade and maintain my skills and receive ongoing clinical supervision.

Professional Experience

I entered the field working for Dr. W. Broadbent, a psychiatrist and director of a large group practice and growth center in Southern California. Dr. Broadbent was supportive and exposed me to many leaders in the field. At the center, I could attend training seminars given by Fritz Perls and many others. After completion of my formal clinical training, I worked with a wide range of populations including mentally and developmentally

(Continued)

Figure 2.10 *(Continued)*

disabled clients. In a CA state hospital setting, I worked primarily in a behavioral mode with a team approach. As Team Leader, I coordinated all professional services for the residents' benefit. My team included a psychiatrist, psychologist, social worker, registered nurse, nursing staff coordinator, and a pharmacist when medication required review.

I left the hospital and created a group counseling practice, *Benicia Counseling Center,* with two colleagues. At the center, I specialized in women's issues and eating disorders; my partner Sigmund specialized in men's issues; and Anna worked with children. We provided clinical services individually, as cotherapists, and as a treatment team. We were often called as expert witnesses and consultants for the courts. My practice consisted of individuals, couples, and families. I also taught psychoeducational classes that included parenting, communication, family stress, and personal leadership. I accepted referrals from managed care companies such as Blue Cross, Champus, and Behavioral Health. I also worked with employee assistance programs such as Chevron in Martinez, California. I provided counseling and consulting services for small businesses in the community to optimize management and staff performance and resolve interpersonal conflicts within high-level management. Other consultation services included organizational development for start-up partnerships, performance problems, and the creation of organizational systems.

Since moving to Boston, I have specialized in eating disorders and women's issues, including posttraumatic stress disorder as it presents in incest survivors, divorce recovery, and victims of abuse. I also provide prevention training through *Personal Organization, Self-Management,* and *Assertiveness Training* classes. I am currently in private practice in Boston's Back Bay and Melrose, Massachusetts. See Current Practice Information and the attached list of behavioral care companies for which I provide services.

Figure 2.11

Sample Specialty Narrative

Susan Froid, LMFT, LMHC
Professional Narrative
Specialty—Eating Disorders

I approach eating disorders in women with a consideration of women's distinctive psychosocial developmental process. I believe that women with eating disorders heal and grow most effectively in a safely constructed therapeutic setting that emphasizes the development of trust in the counselor and the counseling process. Treatment that creates lasting change must honor the individual's life experiences; it collaborates with and draws on the client's cognitive and emotional wisdom to choose what is right for her in the next step in the healing process.

Being a systems-oriented therapist, I believe I must also pay attention to the differing systems the client involves herself with—family; ethnic, racial, and socioeconomic groups; religious groups; and belief systems.

Other aspects of women's lives such as age, presence or absence of children, professional identity and sexual orientation (heterosexual, homosexual, or bisexual) also need to be explored to determine their impact on the development of the eating disorder.

I do not apply a generic treatment methodology to my clients. Consideration is given to the background and circumstance of each eating-disordered woman to provide her with the safety, guidance, and support she needs to recover. I also know I must continually explore and be aware of my own position in relation to my clients (i.e., countertransference and racial, cultural, sexual, or other personal or systemic issues that affect treatment).

Finally, my work is holistic in nature, with attention paid to verbal, nonverbal, and behavioral communications. I also look at the physical, mental, emotional, relational, professional, and spiritual aspects of each client's life.

Figure 2.12

Sample Benefits Statement

Family Therapy

- Increase quality communication between family members.
- Develop strategies for successful conflict resolution.
- Understand the motivation behind children's behavior in order to work creatively with problem behaviors.

Posttraumatic Stress Disorder (PTSD)

- Develop coping skills for intrusive thoughts.
- Learn how to diffuse internal reactions to memories of a past trauma.
- Learn stress reduction techniques that can be used anytime, anywhere.

Treatment Philosophy and Methodology

- Your treatment approach. Many managed care companies prefer a short-term, strategic approach. If you use this approach, be sure to mention it. If not, then provide the rationale for your longer-term methodology.
- Outside resources. It is important to delineate your use of resources such as community groups, agencies, and consultation and referral with other professionals when appropriate.

Fees

- Standard fees for all services.
- Sliding scale stance.
- Fees paid by insurance.

You might also attach a short list of current behavioral healthcare companies that you work with or that have accepted you as a preferred provider.

Access

- Public transportation.
- Handicapped access.
- 24-hour access and emergency plan for acute patients.
- Arrangement for practice coverage in your absence.

New Client Status

- Length of wait for first appointment.

Figure 2.13 provides an example of a Current Practice Information sheet.

The goal of your Practice Information sheet is to let a case manager or colleague understand what kinds of clients you work with and how you approach your work. This helps them make appropriate referrals.

PRACTICE ASSESSMENT

The Practice Assessment is a self-assessment tool that provides a foundation for describing and later developing your practice. I had never completed a practice assessment until I closed a full-time private practice in California. I was considering selling my business and needed to make appropriate referrals for each client. As I reviewed my files and evaluated my office I compiled the information. The final assessment was not surprising, but when it was completed I had measurable proof of what kind of work I was effective at and how my practice could have been improved. When you have completed your assessment, evaluate it for the areas that are undeveloped, or underdeveloped. Create goals in these areas. This will give you the beginnings of a business plan. Now, I do a practice assessment once a year to see what needs to be changed and to evaluate the progress I have made. Figure 2.14 contains a detailed Practice Assessment Worksheet. If you find an area you do not understand, skip it and come back to it after you have read the chapters that follow.

When you have completed the exercises and samples in this chapter, you should have a better sense of the strengths and scope of your practice. The rest of this book will guide you in developing your practice to meet your own professional needs and the needs of your clients.

Figure 2.13

Sample Current Practice Information Sheet

Susan Froid, LMFT, LMHC
Current Practice Information

I am currently in private practice in the Back Bay area of Boston close to the Copley T-exit for easy access by public transportation. My office is wheelchair accessible. I have been in private practice for over 15 years.

Areas of Specialization

Women's issues are my specialty. I follow the work of the theorists who study the psychosocial development of women. Examples of presenting problems are eating disorders, pre- and postdivorce issues, incest, depression, posttraumatic stress reactions, and sexual harassment. I work with victims of abuse and adult children of dysfunctional families. In addition, I counsel professional women who are having difficulty dealing with positions of increased power, are considering career change, or are suffering from performance or leadership problems.

Treatment Philosophy and Methodology

I use a holistic psychosocial, developmental systems approach in working with clients. An assessment is made of each individual's self-development and ego strengths, and then a treatment plan is developed based on the *DSM-IV* multiaxial diagnosis. I promote insight-oriented cognitive restructuring and use strategic behavioral interventions to create change. An extensive history is taken to determine historical and current events affecting the situation and assure a current physical has been taken to rule out organic causes. If there is an organic condition, I work with the physician to create a treatment plan to support medical treatment. When working with couples or families, I provide psychoeducation on how to build and maintain healthy family systems. Communication and conflict resolution skills are also modeled and trained. When working with children who are not able to articulate their feelings and thoughts, I use play therapy and a sandtray. While clients are in treatment, I help them build a support system for themselves and educate them about community resources they might access.

(Continued)

Figure 2.13 *(Continued)*

Fees

My current fees for services are $95/hour for individuals, couples, and families; and $50/group session. Group size ranges from 5 to 10 participants, depending on the focus of the group. Individuals are seen for a 50-minute hour; couples and families are seen for 80 minutes.

Sliding Fee Schedule Since most physicians, dentists, and other health professionals do not operate on a sliding fee schedule, I do not either. I believe a sliding scale undermines the insurance ethics of the profession. I do, however, commit 10 percent of my practice to volunteer counseling and volunteer time working with my local church as a professional resource.

Insurance I accept all carriers who reimburse Licensed Marriage Family Therapists or Licensed Mental Health Counselors. I currently work with managed care and insurances companies both within Massachusetts and those nationally based.

New Clients

I am currently accepting clients for individual work, couples and families. I work with children age 9 and older. I have both day and evening hours available. New clients can usually be seen within three days and emergencies within 24 hours.

Figure 2.14

Practice Assessment and Marketing Planner

The Basics

Date: ____________________

Name: ____________________

Practice Name: ____________________

Type of practice:

Individual	Partnership	Professional partnership
Corporation	Professional corporation	Group on-site
Group without walls	MC entity	EAP
Other: __________		

Address: ____________________

City/State/Zip: ____________________

Phone 1: ____________________

Phone 2: ____________________

Fax: ____________________

E-mail: ____________________

Names and titles of all other practitioners: ____________________

Professional title: ____________________

Professional licenses/certifications: ____________________

Total years in practice: ____________________

Number of locations: ____________________

Years at location(s): ____________________

List all other locations by city and zip: ____________________

About You

Work Relationship Style: _____ Individual _____ Partnership _____ Team

Professional Developmental Stage: ____________________

(Continued)

Figure 2.14 *(Continued)*

About the Practice

Adequate financial accounting system: Y/N
Adequate record-keeping system: Y/N
Records locked behind two barriers: Y/N
Adequate paper-flow (forms) and tracking systems: Y/N
Client-friendly office (easily accessible, comfortable): Y/N
Adequate communication systems (answering system, paging): Y/N
Outcome measures identified and tracked: Y/N
Referral sources tracked and followed up: Y/N
Specialties clearly identified: Y/N
Managed care company tracking systems in place: Y/N
Number of active charts/file: ______________________________
Average number of clients seen weekly: ______________________________
Number of inactive charts/files: Not seen in over a year ___ Not seen in 5 years ___
Mailing list of active clients: Y/N
Of inactive clients: Y/N
Gross fees collected:
  Weekly: ______________________________
  This year to date: ______________________________
  Last year: ______________________________
  Past 5 years: ______________________________
Average number of new patients/clients per month:
  Two years ago: ______________________________
  Last year: ______________________________
  Current year-to-date: ______________________________
Average case size (gross $ spent by a new patient/client in the first 12 months): $_____
Growth Goal (based on current personnel, physical setup, and your managerial abilities, state your gross collection goal for the next 12 months): $ ___________

(Continued)

Figure 2.14 *(Continued)*

Existing yearly promotional budget (yellow pages, newsletters, etc.):

Yellow pages	Newspapers
Newsletters	Signs
Conference presentations	Trade shows
Other ________________	

Total already allocated for next 12 months: $ ____________________________

Initial cash needed (about 50% of the budget will be spent in the first 90 days): $ __________. The same approximate amount will be needed on hand to fund the total promotional budget for the balance of the first year. Months 4–12: $ __________ (50% of $ above)

Sources on hand: _____ Amount: $ _____

Reconcile any differences between goals and budget. Make any adjustments to overly optimistic goals assigned to personnel, physical setup, managerial abilities, and budget. If the projected budget is unrealistically high or low, adjust the budget to a real, realistic number, and adjust the goal accordingly.

Marketing Information

Best sources of new patients/clients in past 12 months:

Yellow pages	Ex-clients	Colleagues
Managed care	Agencies	Public speaking
Trade Show	EAP	Other: __________

List each type of referral from above and the number received over the past 12 months.

Type	*Number of Referrals*

(Continued)

Figure 2.14 *(Continued)*

Review current/recent promotional activities:

Internal Activities:

Newsletters	Direct mail
Other mailings	Other
Special events	

External Activities:

Yellow pages	Public relations
Newspaper or shopper ad	Radio/TV
Seminars	Outdoor office sign
Magazine articles	Other

Indicate return-on-investment (ROI; your income minus cost equals ROI): ____________

Current outdoor office sign: Y/N If not, permission obtainable for one: Y/N

Circle busiest months:

J F M A M J J A S O N D

Circle slowest months:

J F M A M J J A S O N D

Current Yellow Pages listings—

Name(s) and publisher(s): ____________

Size and section: ____________

Monthly cost: ____________

Closing date: ____________

Available Yellow Pages directories that you do not presently use—

Name(s) and publisher(s): ____________

Size and section: ____________

Monthly cost: ____________

Closing date: ____________

(Continued)

Figure 2.14 *(Continued)*

Fees

Date of your most recent price survey in your market: ______________________

Your prices compared with those of competitors:

______ below average ______ average ______ above average ______ high

Date of your most recent increase in prices: ______________________

Amount of increase: ______________________

Basis for determining level of increase: ______________________

Plans

Business plan in place: Y/N

Marketing plan in place: Y/N

Demographics

Approximate population in drawing area for your practice: ______________________

Areas best able to draw from: ______________________

Areas unable to draw from: ______________________

Average annual household income in drawing area:

- ❑ Lower (Under $15k).
- ❑ Middle–lower ($15k–$24k).
- ❑ Middle–upper ($35k–$49k).
- ❑ Upper ($50k and over).

Employment in this area:

- ❑ Minimum wage.
- ❑ Blue collar.
- ❑ White collar.
- ❑ Under employed—highly educated, with little disposable income.

Mostly:

- ❑ Urban
- ❑ Suburban
- ❑ Semirural
- ❑ Rural

(Continued)

Figure 2.14 *(Continued)*

- ❑ Residential
- ❑ Light industrial
- ❑ Heavily industrial
- ❑ Agricultural
- ❑ Downtown business area

Practice Patient/Client Profile

Female ____________		Male ____________	
Age Group		Age Group	
Under 18	______ %	Under 18	______ %
18–29	______ %	18–29	______ %
30–45	______ %	30–45	______ %
46–59	______ %	46–59	______ %
60+	______ %	60+	______ %

Significant ethnic, religious, racial, or foreign language influences: Y/N

List the clients you have seen one year prior to this date by:

Presenting Problems(s) DSM Diagnosis Length of Treatment

For business-oriented practices:—

Industries and/or large businesses: Y/N

Yearly average sales: ____

Estimated number of employees: ____________________________________

Preliminary Market Analysis

Desired market segments (what kind of patient/client you want in your practice. Describe each by sex, age, education, income condition, etc. List by priority):

Segment	*Sex*	*Education*	*Income*	*Presenting Problem*
1.				
2.				
3.				
4.				
5.				
6.				
7.				

(Continued)

Figure 2.14 *(Continued)*

Competition analysis (list main competitors; what do they promote and in what media?):

Competitor	*Promotes What*	*Using What Media*
1.		
2.		
3.		
4.		
5.		
6.		
7.		

Media promotion: Heavy/Light

Primary promotional strengths of the practice that distinguish you as different/better than the competition (rank applicable factors in priority sequence with 1 representing strongest promotional factor; briefly explain key strengths):

______ Professional experience ______________________________

______ Qualifications/credentials ______________________________

______ Broad capabilities ______________________________

______ Special capabilities ______________________________

______ Friendly staff ______________________________

______ Convenient location(s) ______________________________

______ Long-established ______________________________

______ Special equipment ______________________________

______ Large selection of providers ______________________________

______ Lower price ______________________________

______ Financing ______________________________

______ Other (specify) ______________________________

Concise Practice Position Statement

If you could tell the public one statement about your practice that you would want them to remember, what would it be?

What benefits do your clients receive when they use your services? List by specialty or segment.

3

ESTABLISHING A PRACTICE

Professional Person Meets Businessperson = Identity Crisis

A successful professional practice is never what people envision it will be, so prepare for a personal and professional great adventure. As for any journey, you must know where you are going, and what you need to take with you. Two survival skills for this journey are perseverance and a finely tuned sense of humor.

Success for anyone beginning a professional practice is contingent on many ingredients:

- The ability to provide services by adhering to high professional standards.
- The knowledge to create an efficiently operating office.
- The financial skills to remain solvent or economically viable by using sound business practices.

Reaping the personal rewards of success creates demands as well. You must pay attention to, and develop skills for, managing your success.

To begin, assume that you are already successful in the service delivery of your discipline: You are already *clinically competent and technically terrific.* But, you are financially disappearing, or you are interested in a more independent lifestyle. Although you mostly experience yourself as top-notch at your craft, you sometimes feel like a business beginner.

Usually the overt characteristics that attract people to the professions are quite different from the ones that successful businesspeople seem to possess. With a little help and attention, however, you can develop those attributes yourself. The qualities that make you a successful craftsperson—creativity and attention to process and content—can be thought of as your yin; to become a successful businessperson you also must develop your yang, or attention to procedural outcomes and the bottom line:

Professional/Craftsperson = Yin
Entrepreneur/Businessperson = Yang

Answering the following questions will help you set your professional practice objectives:

- What personal values motivate me to start and run a professional practice?
- If I had all the money in the world, what would I do today?
- What will be said at my eulogy and will it have anything to with my work?
- What would I like the eulogist to be able to say?

Making Your Vision a Reality

> Success is getting what you want—
> Happiness is wanting what you get.

You will find that the more concrete your vision is of your future, the more likely it is to unfold. Take time now to create one day in your future by using the worksheet in Figure 3.1. You may be surprised by how you conceive spending your time when you fantasize the future.

There is much for you to do before you open your business doors to the public. Everyone's experience is different, but there are the fundamentals that will help ensure a healthy professional practice.

The Name

Like the parent of a newborn, you must choose a name for your business. Are you planning to be "Susan Froid XXXX (Title)," "Therapy, Inc.," "A Safe Place To Talk," or the "Psychotherapy Institute"? As an individual, you can be any of the preceding titles. You can be a center, an institute, or an agency, even if you are a sole proprietor. The key is not to mislead others into believing you offer something you don't or mislead people through false advertising. If your vision is to be Therapy, Inc., begin now. When you register your DBA (Doing Business As) with the city you are doing business in, you have created your business name.

The Structure of Your Business

You have choices about whether you want to be a sole proprietor (working alone), a partner, or a member of a group, corporation, or whatever business entity your state allows.

Sole Proprietor

This business form can be created by an individual. The easiest setup is to call yourself by your name and use your Social Security number for tax purposes. The only business issues you need to check out are zoning laws for your office location and federal and local business taxes.

Partnerships and Corporations

If you choose to be involved with a partner or group, one of the first most critical things to find out is whether you have similar work philosophies, mission, and purpose. The questions shown in Figure 3.2, *Forming a Practice Group* are ones many groups avoid; if you learn the answers now, you may avoid problems down the road.

After completing individual assessments, members of the group need to develop collaborative answers to all the questions. To build a strong foundation for a good partnership, the members must value everybody's contributions and maintain a continual dialogue between partners. Put all of your agreements in writing and have everybody sign them.

There are three traditional types of profit-making group ownership: corporations, limited

Figure 3.1

A Success Fantasy

This exercise makes your vision of your professional life more concrete. Create the reality of your new life.

I usually begin my day around ______ and finish around ______. Most days I spend ______ hours working, ______ hours playing, ______ hours devoted to myself, ______ hours with friends, family, and loved ones. I usually wear ____________ at home, ___________ at work, and ____________ to play in. I drive a ____________, and it is ____________ dependable and exceptionally ____________. Personally, I have ____________ hair, weigh ______, and look ____________.

The place that I work/spend my day is ____________. My work environment looks like ____________. It is located ____________. To help make my work easier, my office includes ____________. I am especially proud of ____________.

I spend my mornings __________________. For lunch I (be specific who/where/what/why/how long) ________________. I spend my afternoons ________________. The things I like most about what I do are __________________.

Today is payday. I get paid/pay myself every ____________.

Today, I reached a goal. I received a check for ____________.

Since today is a special day, I think I'll ____________.

Often, at the end of the day or after work, I __________________ For dinner, I __________________. Since it's been such a good week, this weekend I think I'll __________________.

My home is (described in detail) __________________.

This year for vacation, I plan to __________________.

With my savings/bonus, I plan to __________________.

I am interested in __________________ and figure the best way to find out more is to ________________. My fitness program involves __________________ and takes ______ hours per day to be effective. I have ________________ friends and spend __________________ hours per week working in my community. I get involved by ____________. My support network is ____________ and involves ______________.

Beyond all these things, it is really __________________ that sustains me and keeps my life in perspective.

Figure 3.2

Forming a Practice Group

Have each member of the group answer these questions individually. Then gather as a group and compare your answers.

- What type of business do I/we have?
- What kind of business structure do I/we want:
  Partnership? Corporation? Other?
- What is my/our mission?
- What are my/our goals?
- What is my/our primary service or product?
- How do I/we manage leadership:
  Hierarchical? Collaborative?
- How much structure do I/we want?
- What are the benefits of my/our services or products?
- Who is my/our competition?
- How are my/our product or services different from the competition?
- What is the key message or phrase that best describes my/our business?
- What is the name of the group?
- How will I/we manage start-up costs?
- Do I/we have a budget for start-up costs?
- What are my/our strengths?
- What are my/our weaknesses?
- What are the obstacles to my/our success?
- What are my definitions of success?
- What is the group's definition of success?
- Do my professional goals and definition of success have a connection to the group's goals?
- How will I/we manage the business planning process?

partnerships, and general partnerships. You can also set up less formal partnerships on a project-by-project basis. A general partnership is formed between two or more equals who share income, expenses, and liability, as defined by a *partnership agreement.* A limited partnership is created to allow certain partners to invest in the business but restricts their liability to the amount of their investment. A corporation is considered by law an individual entity with rights and responsibilities. Of these three types of business operations, incorporation is the most technical and most expensive to set up and manage. Members of a corporation must pay individual and corporate taxes. A solution to this double taxation is to create a subchapter-S corporation. Corporations can be difficult to terminate because they require unanimous consent from all stockholders. You must also keep corporate records, or the corporation can be dissolved. Although many people believe a corporation will protect them from liability, the small corporation's immunity to liability has recently been increasingly compromised by banks and lenders. Some states have limited liability business entities. Check with your state attorney general for information about the business formations that are allowed in your state. A new kind of group is a *virtual group* or a group without walls. It is a collaboration of several professionals at different work sites. Many individual private practitioners can create an organization like Therapy, Inc. and remain in their own offices. I have watched many colleages create treatment groups. It has been my observation that the most successful kind of therapist group over time is the professional corporation. This business structure seems to support long-term success.

The business structure you choose must meet the majority of your needs. Using the information from your self-assessment, ask yourself what form would serve you best today and in the future. In making your decision, you can find help from many sources. You can start by looking at publications and software packages from a legal self-help group called Nolo Press (1-800-992-6656). There is also a series of books covering every state titled *Starting and Operating a Business in (fill in the state).* They are written by Michael D. Jenkins and John F. Curtis, I used *Starting and Operating a Business in Massachusetts* (Jenkins and Curtis, 1985) (call 1-800-228-2275 for information about your state).

Legal Agreements

When you join with others be clear about what your involvement entails. Have it in writing and run the completed paperwork past an attorney. Nolo Press is a great resource for creating these kinds of documents. They have a book on setting up a partnership, a corporation, and more. Give their bookstore a call at the number cited earlier, and tell them what you need. They are very helpful. For the virtual groups, I have included a sample *professional agreement* (Figure 3.3), and for partnerships a *partnership agreement* (Figure 3.4). The professional agreement defines the relationship between independent practitioners working under a common business name. If you choose to use portions of either one, have an attorney review your document to make certain it meets the laws and regulations for your state. The following professional agreement was adapted from one designed by the Metro-Boston Professional Counseling Network-Independent Practitioners.

The Partnership Agreement defines the roles, relationship, and liability of the partners. The partnership agreement in Figure 3.4 is a sample

Figure 3.3

Agreement of Professional Association Associates

This agreement of Professional Association is made this ____________ day of ____________ by and between (group members). The parties hereby form a Professional Association based on the terms and conditions set forth below:

Name

1. The name of the Association is ____________ - Independent Practitioners.
2. The Associates named above are all independent practitioners.

Purpose

3. The purpose of the Association is to provide ____________.

Liability

4. Each party in this agreement is a completely independent practitioner with sole and complete control and responsibility for the care of his/her clients. Each Associate is solely responsible for his/her own practice including but not limited to, the following: fee setting and collection; hours of practice; records and bookkeeping; professional liability insurance; tax liability; billing; location of practice; and all other financial and professional matters.
5. The Associates may agree from time to time to conduct various advertising and other common interest activities under the name of ____________. When this name is used in advertising or promotional materials, whether orally or in writing, it must be accompanied by a designation indicating each person operates independently as follows: ____________ - Independent practitioners.

Decision-Making Process

6. From time to time, decisions will be made by the Associates to facilitate their common interest activities. All decisions will be made by consensus of all Associates.

(Continued)

Figure 3.3 *(Continued)*

Client Notification

7. Each Associate agrees to provide the following information to potential clients in written form and to provide a copy of such to each Associate:

   Your care and treatment is my sole responsibility and under my sole control. I conduct my own counseling and therapy practice individually and independently.

Complaint Notification

8. If a formal complaint is filed by a client or former client to the licensing board or professional association about an Associate based on professional misconduct, notification of such action will be made to the other Associates within 36 hours in writing. The Associates will decide the relationship between the one so charged and the Associates.

Indemnity

9. Each Associate agrees to indemnify and hold the other parties harmless from any liability, loss, costs, claims, damages, or other expenses, including reasonable attorneys' fees, resulting from the acts or omissions of each of the parties.

Principal Location

10. The principal place of business of the Association is where each individual Associate practices.

Duration

11. This Professional Association shall continue until dissolved by mutual agreement.

Finances

12. All financial contributions to the Association shall be made equally by all the Associates.

Management

13. All Associates shall have an equal voice in the management of the Association.

(Continued)

Figure 3.3 *(Continued)*

Assignment

14. Each Associate agrees that he/she may not, and shall never attempt to, assign, pledge, give away, or otherwise alienate his/her interest in the Association or any part thereof.
15. No Associate without the consent of the other Associates shall:
    a. borrow money in the name of the Association;
    b. lease or mortgage any interest in the Association;
    c. enter into any contract, pledge, release guarantee, deed, indemnity bond, or surety bond that bears the name of the Association.

Mediation

16. If any controversy or claim arising out of the Association agreement cannot be settled by the Associates or their legal representatives, such controversy or claim shall be resolved by mediation. The Associates are aware that mediation is a voluntary process and pledge to cooperate fully and fairly with the mediator in an attempt to reach a mutually satisfactory compromise for any dispute.

Scope

17. This agreement contains all of the terms and conditions agreed upon by the parties hereto, and no other agreements, oral or otherwise, regarding the subject matter hereof shall be deemed to exist or to bind any of the parties. This agreement cannot be modified or amended except in writing executed by all of the parties that expresses its terms and its intention to modify the agreement.

Termination

18. Any Associate may terminate his/her participation in this agreement upon giving sixty days prior written notice to the other parties. In addition, this agreement shall terminate with respect to any party upon the termination of the mental healthcare practice of that party due to death, disability, or retirement. While not required hereunder, it is agreed that, whenever possible a party will give the other parties at least four months' written notice of her/his intent to terminate this agreement.

(Continued)

Figure 3.3 *(Continued)*

Business Intentions

19. Nothing in this agreement shall be interpreted as creating any partnership, joint venture, or similar joint enterprise.

In witness whereof, the Associates have signed this agreement of Professional Association:

Date: ____________

Individual Members: __________________

____

____

____

Figure 3.4

Partnership Agreement

This Partnership Agreement is established between the partners listed below:

Sigmund Smith
Susan Froid

The partnership is effective on (date).

1. Name: The name of the partnership is Therapy, Inc.
2. Location: The principal place of business is located at 123 Main Street, Benicia, CA.
3. Duration: The partnership shall continue until terminated in writing by all partners.
4. Purposes of Partnership: The purpose of the partnership shall be to engage in providing psychological services.
5. Contributions:

   Cash: The partners shall contribute an equal share amounting to $500, by January 1, 1997.

   Property: The following property is contributed by:

Name	*Property*	*Valued At*	*Date*

   Services: The following services shall be donated as follows:

Name	*Service*	*Valued At*	*Date*

(Continued)

Figure 3.4 *(Continued)*

6. Allocation of Depreciation or Gain or Loss of Contributed Property: The partners intend that the general allocation rule of the Internal Revenue Code shall apply. Gain or loss shall be allocated proportionately between the partners.
7. Management: Each partner shall participate equally in the management and decision making for the business.
8. Financial Management:

8.1 Accountings: Accountings of all accounts shall be made periodically every quarter from the date of this agreement.

8.1.1 Partner Accounting: An individual capital account shall be maintained for each partner. The capital shall consist of his/her original contribution of capital, and increased by additional capital contributions, services or products, and profits. It will be reduced by his/her share of partnership expenses and losses.

8.2 Salaries: No partner shall receive any salary for services rendered to the partnership except as first approved by each partner.

8.3 Expense Accounts: An expense account, not to exceed $50 per month, shall be set up for each partner. Each partner shall keep an itemized record of expenses and be paid within 30 days of a Request for Payment submitted to the financial manager.

8.4 Signature Required on Partnership Checks: All partnership funds shall be deposited in the name of the partnership and shall be withdrawn only on the signature of both partners.

8.5 Books of Accounts: The partnership shall maintain adequate accounting records which shall be open at all times to inspection by all partners. The books shall be kept on a cash basis.

8.6 Fiscal Year: The books of account shall be kept on a fiscal year basis, commencing on January 1 and ending December 31. The books shall be closed and balanced at the end of each year.

8.7 Annual Audit: The books of accounts shall be audited at the close of each fiscal year by an accountant chosen by the partners.

(Continued)

Figure 3.4 *(Continued)*

9. Meetings: Meetings for the purpose of conducting business and discussing issues of general interest shall be held monthly or at other times agreed upon by both partners.
10. Outside Business Activities: Any partner may not engage in any activity that materially interferes with the business of the partnership.
11. Transfer of a Partner's Interest:
    - 11.1 The Right of First Refusal: Any partner that receives an offer to purchase all or a portion of his/her interest in the partnership shall give written notice of the terms of the offer, identify the proposed buyer, and shall give the other partner the option, within 60 days after the notice is given, to purchase that partner's interest on the same terms as those contained in the offer.
    - 11.2 Internal Sale: If any partner chooses to leave the partnership for whatever reason, or becomes incapacitated he/she or the estate shall be obligated to sell his/her interest in the partnership to the remaining partner for the sum of the accounts held in his/her name by the partnership. No value for goodwill shall be included in determining the value of a partner's interest.
    - 11.3 Election of Remaining Partner to Continue Business: Upon the retirement, death, or disability of a partner, the remaining partner shall have the right to continue the partnership him- or herself or with any other person or persons he/she may select. He/she shall pay to the retiring partner, or to the legal representatives of the deceased partner, the value of his/her interest in the partnership.
    - 11.4 Dissolution of Partnership: If the remaining partner does not elect to purchase the interest of the outgoing partner, or in the event the partners mutually agree to dissolve the partnership, the partnership shall terminate.
    - 11.5 Addition of New Partners: New partners may be added to the partnership only by unanimous written consent of all existing partners.
        - 11.5.1 New Partners Liability: The new partner shall not be personally responsible for any debts of the partnership incurred on or before the date of their partnership designation.

(Continued)

Figure 3.4 *(Continued)*

12. Dispute Resolution: The partners agree that any dispute affecting the partnership business shall first be resolved by mediation. The mediator shall be ____________ or ____________. The costs of mediation shall be shared equally by the partners and any decision reached shall be put in writing and signed by all partners. The mediation agreement shall be binding on both of them.

This agreement shall be binding upon the parties and their successors.

Signed on (date): ________________________

____

____

____

____

Notary: ________________________________

one for two partners. I recommend using the worksheets in *The Partnership Book* (Clifford & Warner, 1993) to personalize your partnership agreement.

Legal Issues

A mental health counselor not only has to be concerned with business and legal issues but must also be knowledgeable about professional practice issues and malpractice. The following tips will keep malpractice issues at bay:

Be Competent. Get the training you need for any specialty you declare.

Use Reasonable Judgment and Operate in Good Faith and Fairness. Many unexpected business issues will come up. When in doubt, talk to others but know the buck always stops with you. Make the fairest ethical decision you can. Make certain you create a written record of how you came to that decision if it is in relationship to any previous or current client.

Don't Experiment with Clients. Research is a noble cause but unless it is planned, documented, and all involvement acknowledged in writing, you shouldn't experiment.

No Sex Never Never Never. No reason will be acceptable.

Consult When Necessary. We are never all things to all people and often run into new situations we need some help with. If your client demands skills beyond your scope of practice, refer or consult with a colleague. Document this decision along with your actions to serve your client's needs.

Don't Abandon Clients. If you are working with a client who can no longer pay or whose managed care benefits run out, you still are responsible for the person. You should have planned ahead if the client had limited benefits. When the unexpected happens, formulate a plan that will help such clients get the services they need. Look for alternate resources in agencies or the public sector. If there are none, create a treatment plan that will help them reach an area of stabilization and establish a support system for when they terminate. Every clinician should address this issue whenever taking on a new client. Don't make a commitment to treat if you are unsure of the funding source or are unwilling to provide pro bono services when benefits run out.

Operate within Your Scope of Practice. When you created your professional narrative and biography, you were describing your qualifications. Your *scope of practice* is described in your licensing or certification laws and guidelines. Always know what your scope of practice is and operate within it. When called to step outside this framework by a client, with no other resources available, always consult and document what you are doing to rectify the problem.

Document Everything. Sometimes we run into old clients or get phone calls unexpectedly in the night. Whenever an event involves a previous or current client, make an entry in the client's file objectively describing what happened and your response.

Support Course of Treatment. If you have made a commitment to a course of treatment to another professional, a managed care organization, or an insurance company, you must support that commitment. If you change your mind, it must be documented and communicated to all involved, including your client.

Maintain Accurate Problem-Oriented Client Records. If you could find a tool with the potential to make you money, save you money, and keep you out of litigation for malpractice, would you consider using it? These are the likely benefits of good professional record keeping. Most attorneys agree that thorough, well-written clinical records can provide an excellent defense against malpractice claims. As a counselor who has been in private practice for many years, I can also tell you that accurate record keeping has made me money because of increased referrals and extended treatment by insurance companies. Inadequate record keeping has lost me money in a contested claim because my records were not as thorough or organized as they should have been.

Confidentiality. Records must be confidential and not available for others' eyes unless legally or clinically necessary. I recommend that you protect your records with three locks. Use a filing cabinet with a lock, placed in a room that also has a lock, to which only you and those with a need to know have keys. The lock on the main door of your office provides the third security device. A password on your computer is also considered a lock.

Record System. Decide how you will keep your records, what format and forms you will use. Your clinical records must be organized and standardized. Organize client information into the following categories:

- Intake sheet.
- Individual and/or family history.
- Evaluations (mental status exam, psychological tests).
- Diagnosis.
- Specific treatment objectives and the methods you will use to reach measurable goals.
- Progress notes.
- Termination summary.
- Supervision/consultation notes.
- Medication records (current/historical).
- Correspondence and legal documents (releases of information).
- Financial information.

Keep your billing records separate from your clinical records. You may need to use your financial records for purposes other than your client's issues and will allow freedom of access to others without jeopardizing your client's confidentiality, (e.g., bookkeeper, secretary, collection agency, tax auditor).

When insurance carriers were polled, the majority stated they expected a standard clinical record with a diagnosis, treatment plan, and dated notes from each session detailing progress. I have also found that it is essential to keep copies of every claim form filed, including notes about follow-up calls to carriers, and attempts to collect copayments from clients. When filling out insurance claims, make sure you specify the procedure codes they are using in their system to authorize payment. Avoid surprises, such as not receiving a check because you submitted a claim number they did not approve for payment.

Problem-Oriented Record Keeping. When you create a client's clinical notes, make certain they are concise. I recommend a problem-oriented system. That means that in the left-hand column of your clinical notes form (a form is better than a blank piece of paper) you enter the date seen and a number that coincides with a problem you identified as one of the treatment issues. Record only clinically relevant behavior, interventions, client responses, and progress in relation to your proposed treatment plan. Try to record your notes as soon after your session as possible and be certain to date and sign all notations at the end of the entry. If more than one person is making entries you should never fabricate a record at a later date. If your records are altered after the fact, it will bring their validity into question in a court of law. Never obliterate a note if you need to make a change; draw a line through it, initial, and date the deletion; and then record a note on the date of change, describing the reason for the change.

Other recommendations are to have a standard procedure for evaluating danger-to-self and others (suicide and homicide risk), child and elder abuse, and other sensitive treatment issues. Note your use of these procedures in your clinical records. You might also consider the standard use of appropriate psychometric indices when necessary to expand and verify the clinical picture of your diagnosis. I have found that treatment interventions that follow directly from published professional theories hold up best in the courtroom. Psychotherapy can be viewed as both a science and an art, but the science side is preferred when the standard of care is up for evaluation in a malpractice claim.

Use clear, objective behavioral descriptions in your notes. Stay away from jargon and personal descriptive terms. One model used in the medical world is the SOAP note. That is Subjective, Objective, Assessment, Prognosis. This provides you an opportunity to include your impressions along with the objective and clinically assessed information as backup.

Maintain Records for Seven Years. Some therapists hold records until they die. All clinicians should arrange with someone to archive their records in case of their death. Include it in your will if your attorney will allow it.

Don't Erase. If you make an error in your notes, simply draw a line through it, write "error," date it, and initial it. If something is erased or covered with correction fluid, it is anyone's guess what was said. When it is still there, no one can accuse you of hiding anything.

Limit Your Practice to a Size You Can Handle. Many clinicians get so busy they begin to make errors in judgment. Some professionals start long waiting lists, which are not in the best interest of the client. Decide how many clients you can attentively see per day and per week and remain balanced in the rest of your life. If you have become so successful that clients wait to see you, make certain you offer them other resources in case there is a long lapse of time and their symptoms get worse. It is their choice then whether to wait for you or get treatment now.

Informed Consent. Every new client needs to be given basic information about the relationship you two (or more) are entering. This information should include:

- Fees.
- Your credentials.
- Collection policies.
- How you handle no-shows.

- Your method of doing therapy.
- Confidentiality.
- How you can be reached outside the sessions.
- What to do in case of emergency.
- What they can reasonably expect from therapy.
- Alternatives to therapy.
- Client rights.
- The consequences of not being treated.

I would also have this checked by an attorney before giving it to clients. Have new clients read and sign this document to show they have read and understand it. Give them their own copy for their files and keep one for yours. When questions covered in this document come up during your professional relationship, refer them back to it.

Seek No Personal Benefit beyond a Reasonable Fee. Clients often want to give you gifts or other outside benefits. The best way to handle these offers is to say no and then deal with the need to give as a clinical issue. Any relationship or benefit outside the counseling office can be viewed as a dual relationship, which is inappropriate in a counseling situation.

Assist Clients in Creating Their Own Outside Resources. Every client benefits from a strong external support system. Make certain you know about community resources and share these with your clients as appropriate.

Terminate Ethically and Appropriately. When a client no longer needs your services, make certain you have created a termination plan. Don't decide today that next week is the last visit. If your client makes this kind of decision, recommend an appropriate termination process. Stopping treatment is the client's choice, of course, but enter into your records that you offered the alternative plan and include the client's response.

Obtain Professional Consultation or Supervision at All Times. Supervision is not something people seek because they are poor therapists. Supervision is a place to stay objective about your work and discover blind spots and new options for treatment. If you are sharing your work with others, you are less likely to wander down the wrong treatment path.

Make an Informed Decision about Carrying Malpractice Insurance. Most behavioral healthcare companies require their panel members to carry malpractice insurance. Professionals who do not work in this arena have the choice to carry it or not. Discuss this issue with colleagues and your attorney. There are many areas of impact if you do or do not choose to carry this protection. Know the details.

Know Laws and Legislation That Affect Your Work. Ignorance of the law is not a good defense. Take whatever steps are necessary to get copies of laws, legislation, and any other guidelines that affect you. This also includes standards of practice and ethical guidelines of your professional association. Changes are made often, so update this information yearly.

MANAGING YOUR OFFICE

Choosing your office location can be dictated by how much money you have or be the result of a professional opportunity. Better yet, it could rest on your having researched the optimal location based on professional saturation and referral resources. If you start up because of low funds or use an easy opportunity, keep in mind there is more to it than that. Begin to gather the information regarding your ideal location. Then, when you are ready, you can make the most of your resources. Some features that clients and managed care companies look for are:

- Handicapped accessibility.
- Parking.
- Good lighting.
- Access to public transportation.
- General safety for your clients.

Your clients will react to the furnishings and general ambience of your office. It is your decision whether or not to have a waiting room. More space costs more money. If you have a waiting room, make sure that it is adequately soundproofed so no one can hear your clients while they are in session. An exit from your counseling office that does not require clients to walk through the waiting room as they leave is a good idea. These are ideals, but if you don't look for them you will never have them. Don't sign a long lease unless you are in your perfect office and then think about it twice. The marketplace will change, and you may decide to change your location.

Security

Record Keeping

If your work is on a computer, you should require an access code or password to obtain client information. If you are using a filing cabinet, it must also have a lock and be behind another lock.

Use standard forms in your client records. Many managed care companies will supply you with the forms they want you to use: Use them. Resources for office forms are:

- *The Paper Office* (Zuckerman & Guyett, 1991). It is also available on a computer disc so you can customize it.
- *The Foundations of Your Private Practice,* Volumes 1 and 2 (Gold,1994).
- Your professional association.

Communication Systems

Make certain your method for taking messages is confidential. If you use an answering machine, don't pick up messages and broadcast them throughout your office while anyone else is there. If you are faxing information about a client check to see whether the receiving FAX is *secure,* or in an area where only right-to-know professionals are present. Don't use a cellular phone to talk about client issues and don't e-mail information unless it is secure. This may sound paranoid, but confidentiality is imperative and technology lends itself to eavesdropping. Many professionals are now wearing pagers. Don't use one unless you respond to the pages quickly.

Computers and Software

With today's complex billing systems, I highly recommend a good computer and software for practice management. Before you buy anything, decide what your needs are and then research the hardware and software available to meet them. Don't buy a system and then try to modify it to your needs. When you buy equipment or software, take the training necessary to use it well, or you are wasting your time and your money.

Many practice management software packages are on the market. I suggest you ask colleagues with the same size practice what they use and whether they are happy with it. If this doesn't lead you anywhere, find someone who will let you use his or her equipment or rent time from someone. Order the demo discs from the software companies and try them out. A good source of additional information on available clinical software programs is *The Mental Health Technology Bible* (Rosen, 1997). This guidebook compares billing, scheduling, and treatment assessment and contains a CD-ROM with demonstrations of many available programs.

Computerizing your office may sound tedious but practice management packages are expensive and you will want to be happy with your purchase. Also, once you have loaded all your client information into a program, you are not going to want to start all over. There are many consultants who will help you buy and install your computer system (check the yellow pages). If you don't have any in your area, call the customer service department of the computer company you have decided to buy from and ask for their consultant list. Most computer companies know of consultants across the nation who help people buy their equipment and install it properly.

I recently reviewed a practice management program that can be used on the DOS and MAC platforms that is comprehensive and easy to use. It is offered by Psychotherapy Finances and is called SumTime.™ Contact them for a demo disc. The system also has an add-on electronic billing module: Some say that in the future, professionals without the capability of electronic billing will be locked out of managed care.

Self-Management

Find some kind of self-management system that works for you. Some people find a simple calendar with their client schedule on it works fine. Others use more sophisticated systems called PINs or *Personal Information Networks.* An example of a hardcopy and software system is the DayRunner™ or Franklin Day Planner®. The Franklin Day Planner® helps you track goals, contacts, and other information. Franklin also has an excellent training program. You can reach them at 1-800-276-5414.

Making and Managing Your Money

Fee Setting

This is a complex issue at best. The most straightforward way to set fees is to do some research in your area and find out what other professionals are charging. If you are new to the business, stay within that ballpark. If you are a seasoned professional, do the same and place yourself on the high end. If you are expanding into new markets, the same drill is called for. If you are consulting, get a book on fee setting for the consultant. A good one is *The Consultant's Kit* (Lant, 1981).

Bookkeeping Systems

Whether you work closely with an accountant, hire a bookkeeper, use an outside bookkeeping service, or handle the books yourself, it is vital to understand the documentation and tracking systems required for monitoring your income and expenses. A good system prepares financial statements, prepares cash flow and budget projections, and determines your tax liability. Effective record keeping will help you manage your practice successfully and avoid costly mistakes. A good fiscal system help you:

- Support items reported on your tax returns.
- Identify the source of a receipt.
- Keep track of your deductible expenses.
- Figure depreciation deductions.
- Take advantage of capital gain and loss laws.
- Figure your earnings for self-employment tax purposes.
- Plan your tax strategies.

If any of the preceding terms are new to you, it is even more important that you begin to educate yourself about the financial aspects of your practice. The pegboard (One-Write™) bookkeeping system is an excellent place to start. Resources for a beginning pegboard system are:

- One-Write Systems 1-800-327-7557.
- SafeGuard Systems 1-800-331-9940.
- Wilmer Systems 1-800-526-6555.
- ASH Accountants' America's Supply House 1-800-342-5274.

Generally, a record-keeping system should contain the following information:

- A client record card on which you note each visit, date, types of service (a procedure code will do), charge, payment, and balance. A two-part client visit slip (voucher) should be filled out for each appointment.
- A record or day sheet of all financial transactions, including client name, services rendered, fees charged, and payments received. The day sheet and your appointment book or schedule sheet often can be combined. This is the client control journal.
- A system to account for and safeguard daily cash income, petty cash, and change funds.
- Bank deposit slips listing all cash and checks for a period (daily is best but semiweekly is acceptable if practice receipts are small) reconciled to client vouchers for the period and a day sheet for the period backed up with calculator tapes.
- A *paid bills* file that organizes all paid invoices alphabetically. All business expenses should be paid by a business check with the invoice backup. Keep cash receipts and cash disbursements journals listing each activity classified by appropriate income and expense categories.

These records provide information needed to prepare financial statements and summaries. All business transactions are recorded chronologically in a daily or general journal. Information from the journal is periodically posted to the permanent ledger, which groups transactions by asset, liability, owner's equity, income, and expense accounts.

Periodic financial statements, income statements, and balance sheets are prepared from the month-end summaries or ledger. Monthly income statements are used to analyze the sources of income and expenses. The balance sheet provides a financial picture of the assets, liabilities, and net worth of your practice at a specific time. Both financial statements are required at least once a year for tax purposes and when applying for a loan.

The dollar figures from the income statement also may be calculated as percentages of the total gross income. If you use percentages, or operating ratios, you can see what portion of your income is spent running the practice. Operating ratios may be used to compare performance during one accounting period with that of previous time periods or to compare with industry averages.

Types of Record-Keeping Systems

The systems and equipment that you may use for record keeping can range from simple and inexpensive manual procedures to more costly computer systems. A pegboard system is used by most solo practitioners starting a new practice. Such a system allows you or your assistant to enter a business transaction onto several forms, a visit slip, ledger card, daily journal all at the same time by using carbon or NCR (no carbon required) paper. The forms are aligned on a board and held in place with pegs. After recording the transaction, you advance the forms a notch on the board, making them ready for the next entry. This system minimizes the number of steps required for each transaction, thereby reducing the possibility of errors and saving time. These systems come in a variety of forms. Representatives from accounting system supply houses can help you choose a system best suited to the needs of your practice.

A computerized system provides essentially the same information that a manual record-keeping system does. It has the added advantage of being able to organize data, project multiple future scenarios, and produce hypothetical or test cases given various conditions. Depending on the type of computer system you own or buy (Apple or DOS based), several packaged psychotherapy-oriented systems are available with a wide range of features and costs. Quickbooks™ operates on both platforms and is fairly user friendly. If you decide to computerize your books, take the tutorial or training you need to keep them accurately. Considerable time can be wasted and money lost with messy books. The best time to set this up is in the beginning. Your system will need to track copays, payments from more than one insurance company, collections, partial payments, and payments plans. Use the system that supports record accuracy.

Collections

If you offer your services in good faith and there is a clear agreement about what they cost, your client is responsible for paying you. Collections are something you can do in-house or refer out to a collection agency. If you choose to go out of house, ask your colleagues which agency they use and whether they are satisfied with the service. If no one has a referral, call up the listings in the yellow pages and ask them if they do now or ever have handled mental health practices. Find out what their policies are before you send them a case. Also check out with them the kind of information that facilitates quick and painless collection. Put the questions in your intake form to get the needed information. It is much easier to get a person's driver's license number and Social Security number the first day than when the client has stopped making payment on a bill.

Budgets

Budgets may seem boring but they are worth the effort. When you know how much money you need to earn to support yourself and your business, you are more motivated to do what it takes to bring in the business. Make simple budgets for yourself. For a start-up business, consider how much you will need for setting up an office.

Rent
Furniture
Utilities
Telephone
Answering system
Business stationery
Computer and software
Office supplies
Liability insurance
Attorney fees
Consultant fees

Once you have this covered, consider your ongoing general operating expenses. These include:

Rent
Telephone
Utilities
Answering system
Insurance
Business operations
Client expenses
Professional dues
Insurance
Taxes—local, state, federal
Consultants
Bookkeeping
Attorney fees
Commuting costs
Supervision
Continuing education
Books and publications
Retirement funds
Networking costs

You can use the worksheet in Figure 3.5, *Business Budgets,* to create your start-up and operating budgets. These will help you determine how many clients, and at what fees, you need to stay in business.

Billing and Tracking Insurance

To bill insurance companies, you need an understanding of the *Diagnostic and Statistical Manual of Mental Disorders (DSM-IV;* American Psychiatric Association, 1994) billing and procedure codes. If you purchase a practice management system, these should be included. If you are using a paper system, you can purchase workbooks from the Medical Arts Press (tel. 1-800-328-2179) to help you. The current *DSM* can be purchased from the American Psychiatric Press, Inc. (tel. 1-202-682-6288).

Hiring Experts

If you have a business or clinical need for professional advice and can't find the appropriate expert, go to your professional association or local chamber of commerce. You are not alone and are probably not the first one to run into your particular problem. Reach out to your available resources. It is much better not to feel alone in this business—get the best expert advice possible.

Figure 3.5

Budgets

Start-Up

Item	*Cost*
Rent	$ ______
Furniture	$ ______
Utilities	$ ______
Telephone	$ ______
Answering system	$ ______
Business stationery	$ ______
Computer and software	$ ______
Office supplies	$ ______
Liability insurance	$ ______
Attorney fees	$ ______
Consultant fees	$ ______
Total Start-Up Costs	$ ______

Monthly Operating Costs

Item	*Monthly Cost*
Rent	$ ______
Utilities	$ ______
Telephone	$ ______
Answering system	$ ______
Insurance	
Professional	$ ______
Liability	$ ______
Fire	$ ______
Office expenses	$ ______

(Continued)

Figure 3.5 *(Continued)*

Item	*Monthly Cost*
Client expenses	$ ______
Professional dues	$ ______
Insurance	$ ______
Taxes—local, state, federal	$ ______
Consultants	$ ______
Bookkeeping	$ ______
Attorney fees	$ ______
Commuting costs	$ ______
Supervision	$ ______
Continuing education	$ ______
Books and publications	$ ______
Networking and entertainment costs	$ ______
Retirement funds	$ ______
Miscellaneous	$ ______
Total Monthly Expenses	$ ______

Divide Total Monthly Expense by your hourly rate. That will tell you how many client hours you need just to meet your monthly expenses.

Total Monthly Expenses $ ______ ÷ $ ______/Hour = ______ clients/month

Consulting with Individuals and Business

One of the new roles many professionals are moving into is that of the professional consultant. Mental health professionals possess a vast knowledge of how people and people systems work. They are an invaluable asset to the business arena. Businesses, on the other hand, will want to know in pragmatic terms just what you can offer them and how it will help them be more productive and save money. Your tasks become articulating what you have to offer in understandable terms and demonstrating how this service will benefit your new customer. The process-oriented therapist needs to translate the contextual approach into a procedural benefit-oriented description.

There are many excellent books to help you understand this new role and make the change. An important new skill is how to charge for your services. Some professionals continue to charge at an hourly rate. Many businesses will want you to cost out a project or particular service. There are new skills to be learned, such as setting up consultation contracts and establishing a different fee structure. A book I have found helpful is *The Contract and Fee-Setting Guide for Consultants and Professionals* (Shenson, 1990). Shenson takes you through the process of setting a fee, writing a proposal, drafting a contract, tracking your progress, submitting the final report, and collecting your fees. Of all the new directions the mental health professional can take, this is one of the most challenging with a potential for great reward. You have an opportunity to reach many more people and become a prime mover in the marketplace. If you want to change the world, I highly recommend becoming a consultant to big business. If you are thinking of transitions to the corporate culture, you may find the book *From Couch to Corporation* (Martin, 1996) helpful.

The following information on proposals and contracts can help you get started.

PROPOSALS, CONTRACTS, AND FEE SETTING

Proposals

A proposal is the vehicle you use to obtain consulting services. A good proposal will help you clarify what you want to offer a prospective customer and begin the business relationship. A proposal is actually a marketing tool that displays your knowledge in your area of specialization. The document needs to be worded so the potential client can understand what is proposed, but not with so much detail that it eliminates the need for your consulting services. Don't solve the problem in your proposal. Your proposal needs to convince your client that it is important to retain your services. You may find that sophisticated clients will pay for the proposal effort. You can have two layers of proposal. As the first step in consultation, a short piece proposes a full-scale proposal. The first proposal can contain a needs analysis and general proposal development, and the follow-up contract can contain the working proposal. In the body of your proposal use action verbs such as design, determine, analyze, evaluate, administer, and assess. It is a good idea to use a flowchart showing the consultative process (see Figure 3.6 for an example).

The proposal generally includes an evaluation step, capabilities section, and statement of assurances showing how you will get the job done and how you will handle legal or other liability

Figure 3.6

Project Flowchart

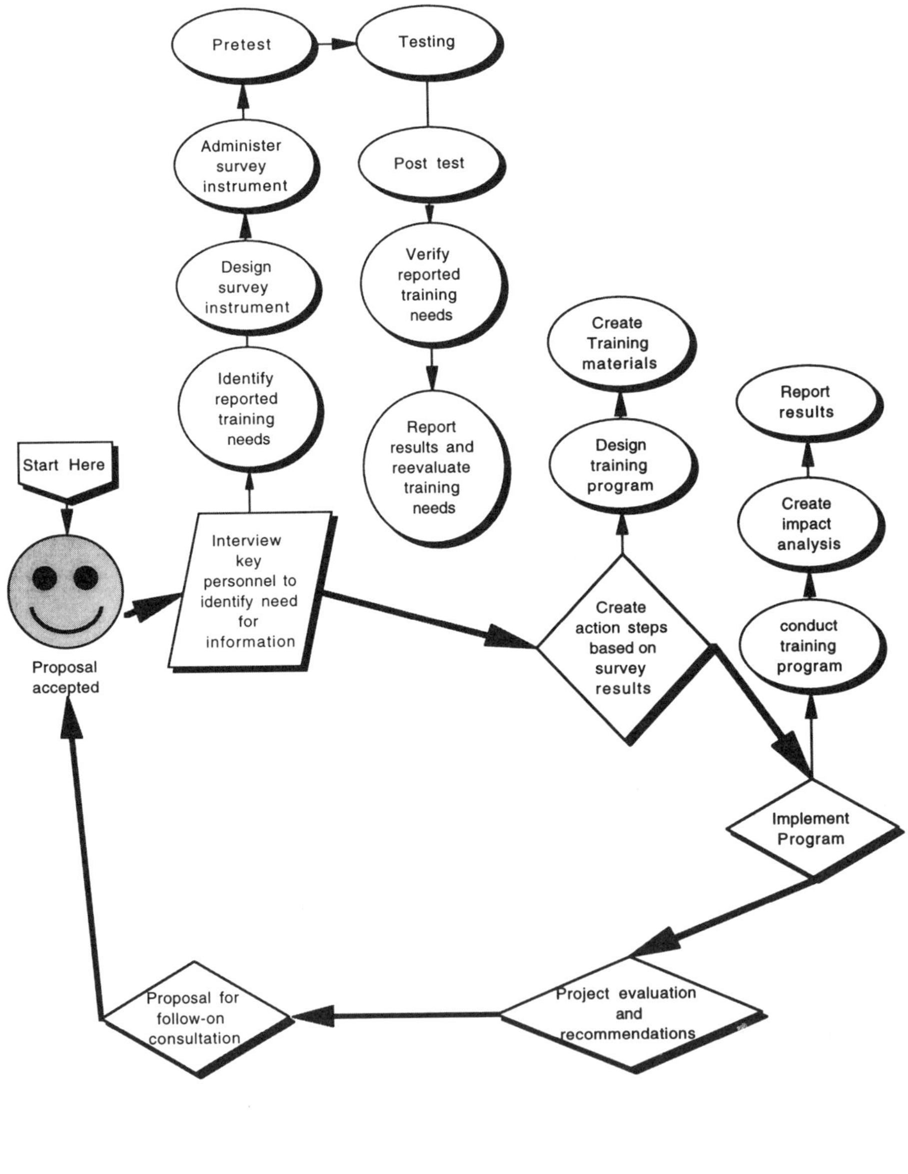

Figure 3.7

Steps in Writing a Client Proposal

1. Talk to the representatives of your prospective client and determine what their problems and needs are and what they expect your consultative services to provide them with.
2. Write a statement of their needs and expectations.
3. Create a statement of goals to come out of the consultative relationship.
4. Break your goals into smaller objectives.
5. Using your needs assessment, goals, and objectives, create a big-picture concept of the consult and a developmental plan for its progression.
6. Create a timeline.
7. Develop an evaluation procedure and reporting plan.
8. Create a capabilities section, or what you will bring to the consultation in terms of your skills and expertise.
9. Develop a statement of assurances to cover any liability or legal problems that might come up.
10. Create a proposed budget with a disclosure strategy that allows your client to understand how and why services and products are priced in a fair manner.
11. Close the proposal with a summary or abstract of the entire document.

issues. Finally, you will propose a budget with supporting information that shows how you determined your fee in the service of getting the project done. Proposal writing goes through a developmental process, as detailed in Figure 3.7.

After creating the document, design your follow-up strategy to take place after the proposal is delivered to the client. If the proposal is rejected, try to determine why. Is it salvageable with this client? If not, can you do something different in the future? If the proposal still does not spark interest, submit it to this client's competitors or others in the field. If it is accepted, you will enter contract negotiations.

Howard Shenson, in *The Contract and Fee Setting Guide for Consultants and Professionals* (Shenson, 1990), takes each step and breaks it down into finer detail for the first-time proposal writer. For someone who is new to the consulting game, creating a proposal is a great way to begin to get a sense of what you want to offer. Try not to take it personally if you are turned down. Use the experience as an opportunity to gather more information for your next proposal.

Writing proposals is a skill just like anything else. The best way to get good at it is practice.

Contracts

Every "how-to" book I read has some sort of disclaimer advising me that the contract information the author is giving me "is not a substitute for your attorney" (Shenson, 1990). My suggestion is to use reference books and self-help legal resources until you feel comfortable with your contract; then pay for an hour's appointment with an attorney who works in the arena addressed in your contract. I always ask my potential clients if they have a standard contract they prefer to use. Armed with all this information, I call the attorney I have identified as my best resource and make an appointment. This kind of preparation saves you time trying to figure out what an attorney said after you have left his or her office. It also provides a base of understanding to ask questions during your hour. I believe the same process for choosing a therapist stands for choosing attorneys. They should have expertise in the area where you seek advice and you should feel that you have a good, trusting relationship with them.

Types of Contracts

There are many kinds of contracts. You can have a formal written contract, a letter of agreement, or a verbal agreement. As you can guess, the formal written contract is the clearest for both parties.

Flow of Information

There is a general contract formula. It starts with the introduction covering the background for the contract and basic assumptions. Following that is the basic agreement between the parties, then a scope of the services you will be providing. Finally, the contract states how both parties will be protected from liability, fees, and any special considerations. Both parties sign it. Often it is notarized. Any changes to a formal written agreement must be in writing.

Fee Setting

There are different forms of fee setting. Most mental health professionals are used to the hourly rate and are comfortable with sliding-scale models. In the consulting business, there are more to choose from. Here are just a few, but they cover the basic kinds of agreements you can consider as you begin your consulting business:

- *Fixed-Price Contract.* This contract is as simple as it sounds. You provide a service and product for a set fee. That's it.
- *Fixed Fee plus Expenses.* You charge your set fee plus your expenses. This is for more than one day of work. Expenses should be identified beforehand so you don't have any surprises when you submit your bill and your client says the company won't pay for something you were counting on.
- *Daily Rate.* You determine your cost for an entire day. I have also found it valuable to create a half-day rate. The half day is higher than half a full day since it usually eats up the whole day anyway.
- *Daily Rate plus Expenses.* This is the same concept as fixed fee plus expenses.
- *Time and Materials.* This is similar to the daily contract. The consultant pays for expenses and adds a handling charge that can

include secretarial services, work done at the office, or other contracted labor.

- *Retainers.* The consultant makes services available to the client as their need arises. You must determine the client's needs or put a cap on services performed within a set period. Your client may want to establish a minimum level of service for that time.

THE BUSINESS PLAN

Just as a resume can help you win the interview that lands you a job, your business plan is the single most critical document in getting your new business financed and operable. The business plan serves two important purposes:

1. A business plan is your tool to convince investors that you and your venture are worth sinking their money into. It's the coin of the investor's realm. If you want capital, it costs you a business plan.
2. Your business plan serves as your guidebook for the first two years of your business. Your plan must be thorough, well thought out, detailed, and reflect what you can do when you're turned loose on the world. Your business plan will chart your business purpose, providing a blueprint for growth and serving as a baseline to evaluate your practice's success or failure.

You won't follow your plan slavishly—unanticipated conditions will arise, and you'll adjust. You may not make money in your first year or two, but you need to know if you're progressing satisfactorily toward profits. By comparing your results each month with your business plan's projections, you can gauge your success.

Update your plan regularly. Don't scrap your business plan once your business is operating. Update it at least once a year. Keep an eye on the future and where you want to take your practice. You will find that updating will be easier than writing the original, but just as important. You'll know whether your practice has seasonal cycles. Updating the business plan will present new challenges to keep you interested in your future success.

The business plan contains:

- Information about the business.
- Management plans.
- Financial facts.
- Market analysis.
- Marketing strategy.

I prefer to structure the business plan in two sections: the basic business information and the marketing plan. The marketing plan is covered in more depth in Chapter 5. Figure 3.8 contains an outline to help you construct your business plan.

Having all your business systems in place will leverage you into success. Many professionals start their business step by step without ever looking at the whole picture to see what the business requires. This approach limits your growth and can put you in awkward situations. With solid business systems as a foundation, you are positioned to successfully take your services and products to the marketplace.

Figure 3.8

Business Plan Outline

Business Summary

Business description: A description of your ideal professional practice.

Mission: A general statement of purpose.

Name: Your name or DBA (Doing Business As).

Type of business and its services and/or products.

Main message

How does your client benefit from your services? Create three benefit statements for each service offered.

Primary customer profile

Demographics: Age, income, sex, marital status, size of household, education, nationality, geographic location, diagnosis, specialty, socioeconomic factors.

Psychographics:

Values.

Lifestyle habits.

Offerings

Services.

Products:

How do your services or products differ from others?

What is your USP (Unique Selling Principle)?

How are products aligned to services?

History

If your business is new, say so. If you have been around for awhile discuss:

The age of the business.

Prior owners or partners.

How it was acquired.

(Continued)

Figure 3.8 *(Continued)*

Length of time operated by you.
Image or reputation.
Last year's gross income and profit.
Any significant events that have affected your company's development.

Current marketplace:
- Current state of your industry.
- Key success factors in the industry.
- Current competition.
- Your competitive advantage.
- Experience.
- Innovation.
- Sophistication.
- Research.

Future projections.

Past and future demand.

Evolution of the marketplace.

Goals are specific and measurable.
- Short-term goals:
  - Number of new clients per month.
  - Average fee per month.
  - New referral sources per month.
  - Expansion of specific services offered.
- Long-term goals:
  - Number of new clients per month.
  - Average fee per month.
  - New referral sources per month.
  - Expansion of specific services offered.

(Continued)

Figure 3.8 *(Continued)*

Rationale for business:
- Why you believe in your business.
- Why your business will be profitable.
- The future growth opportunities.
- What you have learned about your type of business.

Legal structure:
- Sole proprietor.
- Partnership.
- Corporation.
- Group without walls.
- Limited liability.

State licensing requirements and your status.

Zoning requirements.

Insurance requirements.

Health code requirements.

Business laws and regulations.

Type of lease ownership of your building.
- Does your building need repairs and what are the maintenance costs?

Legality of Trademark, patents, licenses, and copyrights.

Location and facility description.

Geographic market boundaries.

Physical dimensions of office.

Access to public transportation.

Parking.

Security.

(Continued)

Figure 3.8 *(Continued)*

Hours of operation.

Personnel.

Inventory, supplies, suppliers, and equipment.

Economic factors and accounting issues:
- How does your business make money?
- How are your fees and prices determined and by whom?
- What financial records are or will be kept and by whom?
- Three-year financial projections and goals.
  - Number of new clients per month.
  - Average fee per month.
  - New referral sources per month.
  - Expansion of specific services offered.

Management Plan

Basic operating philosophy.

Organizational chart.

Duties and responsibilities of key members.

Resumes of top management.

How salaries and benefits will be set.

What jobs will be added and when.

Salary and benefit budget.

Activities to be done in-house and those to be contracted out.

Relationship to critical referral sources or suppliers in the industry.

Operating plan and schedule of upcoming work for the next one to two years.

(Continued)

Figure 3.8 *(Continued)*

Organizational systems design:
- Paper flow design.
- Records storage.
- Information filing systems.

Manufacturing flowchart for products.

Financial Data

Start-up budget or current operating budget.

List of capital equipment.

Financial statements:
- Tax reports from previous years.
- Balance sheet.
- Income statement.
- Accounts receivable and aging.
- Accounts payable and aging.
- Debt schedule.
- Profit and loss.

Planned purchases:
- Equipment.
- Software.
- Facilities.
- Physical improvements.

Three-year financial cash-flow projections.

Sources of money:
- Where the money will come from for business start-up.
- Where capital investment comes from if you are currently operating at a loss.

4

ANALYZING YOUR SERVICES

The Basket Maker's Story

What Is Marketing?

What is marketing, where did it come from, and why should you care? What's the difference between marketing and selling? Marketing provides a context for developing a business relationship. Selling is the tactical exchange of products and services for fees. As you develop your marketing approach, you will clarify what you do and identify the market segment that can benefit from your offerings. In previous chapters, you started marketing yourself with your practice narrative and practice description. As you proceed through the following chapters, you will include the more elusive ingredients that make you a valuable resource to your customers.

Understanding the origins of marketing and how we developed our present market economy will help you understand your place in the picture. In the following narrative, I have translated the basics of the marketing profession into an enjoyable, people-focused format for mental health professionals.

In the Beginning

In primitive societies, each family unit provided most of its own material needs. Products like food, shelter, and garments were created by the family. Individual needs were predictable, and basic resources were often scarce. When the immediate family could not provide one of these essentials, they socialized with someone who had the commodity and was willing to barter it. The barter system was time-sensitive: First, there was the identification of the need, then the search for the new resource, development of a relationship with the individual or clan that had the resources to fill the need, and finally negotiations for the term of the barter.

Gradually, people developed ways to get what they needed in a less time-intensive manner by using *money, specialization,* and *markets.* Money provides a way to exchange goods, quantify the transaction, and depersonalize it. No longer does there need to be a relationship, only the money that represents the service or product. Specialization makes it easier for an individual and a society to locate what they need. It allows individuals to put their time into what they do well rather than struggling to do everything themselves, even if they are inexpert at a task.

The marketplace was a natural outgrowth of money and specialization. It provided a central location where people could procure many of the things they needed. The specialists who came to the marketplace to sell their products conceived the first marketing principles and were the founders of the entrepreneurial spirit. When two basket weavers were in the same marketplace, why would a customer buy one basket rather than the other? To solve this problem, a weaver might make specialized baskets for specific needs. In a saturated market, each weaver would try to convince customers that his or her baskets were the most desirable ones even though they served the same function as their neighbors' baskets. The first weaver's baskets might be stronger, cheaper, or dyed to match the customer's tepee.

With this scenario, marketing became more complex. The basket maker began to do market research: Who buys his baskets, and why? Who is buying the neighbors' baskets and why? How can he develop baskets that meet the basket buyers' needs more effectively? Maybe he could put his baskets in other places in the market or village to get to basket buyers before the competition does. Most important, how can the weaver communicate to buyers why his baskets are the best and persuade them to lay their money on the table?

Most human service professionals engage in *social marketing.* Social marketing refers to marketing skills that translate the process and outcomes of the transfer of knowledge and help people use this information in healing, wellness, or increased performance. Marketing includes everything you do to grow a professional practice. Marketing is involved in meeting people, working with groups, writing communications, and developing business partnerships.

You've Been Doing It All Along

Marketing includes developing a good reputation by highlighting your strongest professional skills. A good marketing plan sets the stage for you to define those qualities and showcase them. This task would be simple if things always stayed the same, but we live in a rapidly changing marketplace because our society and economy are highly complex. To be a successful marketer, you need to anticipate and prepare for the next change, rather than react to it. Marketing must be an ongoing practice.

Marketing is a social science concerned with the behavior of individuals as consumers. Many professionals, however, view it as solely the misleading offerings of businesses that try to capitalize on, or manipulate consumers.Whenever I used to hire marketing consultants to help me develop my practice, I always felt we spoke different languages. As I look back, I see I was right. I have found value in learning traditional marketing concepts and translating them into ethical tools that are useful for mental health professionals.

Developing a Good Reputation

Establishing a good reputation is a basic marketing essential that professionals usually accomplish without conscious effort. Most professionals have no problem with the following practices:

- Maintaining ethical standards of conduct.
- Being available when clients reach out.
- Referring to others when the need arises.
- Being on time.
- Continuing their education and expanding their areas of expertise.

The following sections describe marketing attributes that are often underdeveloped.

Finding Your Niche

Professionals often get trapped into following where the profession leads, rather than watching where the marketplace is moving and finding a place in it. When a business loses touch with its customers, it is doomed. When the profession loses touch with the needs of the community, everybody loses. The professionals are underutilized and not valued for their skills, and the public cannot access a rich resource.

Network, Network, Network

Professionals often get isolated in their practice and don't go out and meet other professionals. When they do make the effort, they gravitate toward people in their own specialty. Mental health professionals need to meet people in other arenas from whom they might learn and who could become possible business resources.

Prospecting

When professionals see a dysfunctional or ineffectual human process at a meeting or other gathering, they are often reluctant to go to whoever is in charge and suggest their services. Offering to consult and help people with communication, mediation, or teamwork skills is not unethical or an insult to others when properly framed.

Maintaining Visibility

Most professionals keep a low profile and do not try to be visible in the business community. This is a lose-lose situation. Mental health professionals often have to deal with the stigma our culture places on mental illness. What better way to educate people and change this problem than to become more socially involved and educate people on a one-to-one basis?

Get into Print

Most professionals believe they don't have enough time to write for newsletters or magazines, and yet they have many wonderful ideas to share with their colleagues and the public. This is something mental healthcare practitioners just have to make time for.

Join the Information Superhighway

Many humanistically oriented professionals feel intimidated by computers or other technology. They remain technologically challenged, valuing their human relationships at the expense of staying in touch with new forms of connectivity. The expanding information networks are serving many needs and providing new forms of information. You can continue to ride your horse, but someday you will get sideswiped by a fast car. Educate yourself and join the information revolution.

Developing Partnerships

Professionals often have sole practices and find it difficult to visualize collaborating with others. They may fear they will lose control of the way they practice or just won't have the time to put into these new group relationships. The rewards are invaluable in the new connections and the learning that takes place through others.

Change and Enhance

Most professionals continue to provide the same services year after year. Even when their field changes its treatment approaches and they educate themselves about these changes and apply them, they usually do not inform the public of the improvement in their services. To learn and grow is a sign of wisdom, a quality professionals can honor.

Proving Your Worth

Outcome studies show the good job professionals are doing, yet few take the time to gather the information. Many managed care companies will make this kind of information required for new panel and even current panel members. Begin now to find a way to gather this information in a way you feel good about.

Marketing Myths

Myth 1. There is one magic marketing solution.

Most people not involved in marketing mistakenly award it some magic or rainmaker mythology. The truth is that there is no one answer to marketing. Answers vary from person to person and region to region. The only magic is good planning and perseverance.

Myth 2. I don't need to get involved in marketing since my practice is currently full.

It is easy to feel complacent and safe when things are going well. It's generally when things take a turn for the worst that people wake up. Denial in the mental health profession is rampant. Many believe that their reputation or degree will always keep them successful. In a time of rapid change and ever-increasing competition, patient loyalty and many letters after your name will not ensure future success.

Myth 3. Marketing requires a compromise of one's ethics and integrity.

Marketing is the act of educating others about what you do. Simply telling your neighbor what you do is marketing. When you are proud of your work, you enjoy telling others about it. If your marketing is authentic and honest, you will not compromise your ethics.

Myth 4. I only need to market when I start something new or when my practice caseload gets low.

Marketing needs to be a way of life. If it is a one-shot effort, there will be a one-shot response. To avoid wide swings in referrals, marketing must be done often. Referrals you have today may be bought up or leave the marketplace. Good marketing, like the cultivation of a garden, needs to be done regularly to maintain peak productivity.

Myth 5. Word-of-mouth marketing about my expertise and training will assure success.

You can be the best therapist in the world but if no one knows about you except the few people you have served, your professional future is insecure. With more people looking to their health insurance to pay for mental illness, there are fewer out-of-pocket resources. Successful practitioners must continue to explore and develop market resources beyond word of mouth.

KNOWING YOUR MARKET

Where do you begin to understand the marketplace? The best place is with the consumers themselves. Here is a framework with which to consider individuals.

The Players

The Economic Human

This individual carefully evaluates each purchase and orders his or her consumption toward maximum need satisfaction within an identified budget. Almost no one can pretend to be this mythical individual. The continuum ranges from the ideal spender to the totally outwardly driven impulse buyer. Marketers try to generalize the whole range of buyers through social, economic, and psychological profiles to identify their target market.

The Consumer

The consumer is the target of all marketing activities. Theoretically, the producer or provider's major concern should be supplying the consumer's needs. We have evolved, instead, into a culture that is focused on turning the consumer's head and pocketbook in the direction of the producer or provider, giving marketing and advertising a bad name. Most professionals consider marketing a dishonest endeavor and would prefer to avoid it entirely at the cost of their profession. Chapter 5 will provide you with a way to market services that meets both the needs of the professional and those of the consumer.

UNDERSTANDING THE CONSUMERS AND THE FORCES THAT AFFECT THEM

How does an ethical professional approach the marketplace? The successful marketer needs to understand the decision-making process—why people buy, why they don't buy, where they buy. The successful professional needs to think about his or her clients as consumers as well as "presenting problems" or a DSM IV diagnosis.

A model in the service of the consumer that I have found easy to understand is Maslow's (Maslow, 1972) *needs hierarchy*. I also find it helpful to combine this hierarchy with the concepts of values assessments and inner- and outer-directed styles.

Values and Needs

Abraham Maslow's (Maslow, 1972) needs hierarchy is taught in most graduate psychology programs and can be easily applied by professionals. Maslow believed that lower unsatisfied needs pushed higher-level needs into the background. People progress from the lowest physiological needs, from safety and security, to belongingness and love, to self-esteem, and finally to the need for self-actualization. Maslow's theory was combined with the inner- and outer-directed approach by a social scientist Arnold Mitchell in 1978 (Gropp, 1982, pp. 1–7). This combination identified buying habits and lifestyles based on needs, values, and an inner or outer influence perspective. The combined model is called VALS (values and lifestyle segments). The population segments identified are:

Need Driven

- *Survivors* (4% of the population) older, intensely poor misfits, who are fearful and depressed.
- *Sustainers* (7%) live on the edge of poverty, are angry, resentful, streetwise, and involved in the underground economy.

Outer Directed

- *Belongers* (39%) are older more traditional, conventional, patriotic, and sentimental.
- *Emulators* (8%) are youthful, ambitious, want to be seen, are aggressively trying to break into the system.
- *Achievers* (20%) are middle-aged, prosperous, self-assured leaders, and are materialistic. They are considered builders of the "American dream." They are also stable, sentimental, and intensely patriotic.

Inner Directed

- *I-Am-Me* (3%) population is in a transition state showing exhibitionism, narcissism. They are very young, impulsive, dramatic, experimental, and actively inventive.
- *Experiential* (6%) are youthful seekers of direct experience. They are person-centered, artistic, and strongly oriented toward inner growth.
- *Societally Conscious* (11%) are the mission-oriented leaders of single-issue groups. They are considered mature and successful with lives of voluntary simplicity.

Combined Outer and Inner Directed

- *Integrated* (2%) are psychologically mature with a large field of vision. They are tolerant, understanding, and have a sense of being a piece of the whole.

The VALS model is developmental and believes people move up a hierarchy, each successive stage growing out of an earlier stage.

Studies show that contemporary individuals seem to be moving away from the traditional outer-directed stance to the inner-directed preference. This trend is apparent in the fashion industry, which is struggling to keep up with the varied preferences of consumers. No longer can designers dictate what the new season's look will be. Now they must go to the streets and see what is taking place before they go to the drawing tables. Figure 4.1 is a composite of the VALS research and inner- and outer-directed development.

This model is helpful when identifying your target market. When you identify your ideal client, look at the market segment you believe such individuals fall into. This will help you understand how to reach them. Another study done to identify market segments was cosponsored by the Fetzer Institute and the Institute of Noetic Sciences. The outcomes were reported in the *Noetic Sciences Review* (Ray, 1996). The study shows that the United States is stratifying into three cultural segments or worldviews. They are the Heartlanders, or traditionalists (29% of the population); the Modernists, who

Figure 4.1

Hierarchy of Needs Developed with Inner and Outer Focus

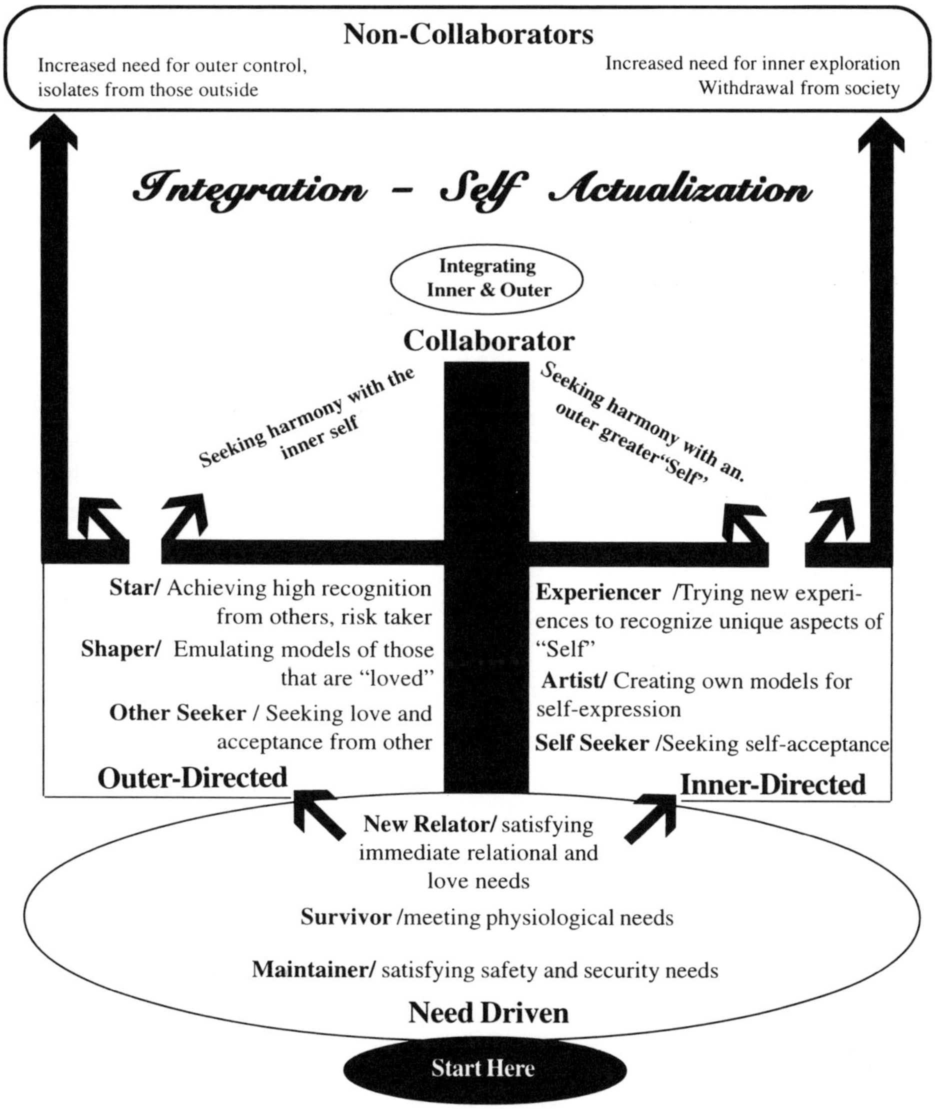

value science, technology, and industrialism (47% of the population); and the new Cultural Creatives, who value ecological sustainability, globalism, women's issues, relationships and family, altruism, self-actualization, alternative healthcare, spirituality, and spiritual psychology (24% of the population). When you are identifying specialties, keep in mind that the behavioral healthcare industry will be pursuing every marketplace possible with many advertising dollars. You need to identify a niche for yourself that does not fit into the managed care model. With your unique niche, you have more time for your marketplace to remain unexploited by big business. The Cultural Creatives fit this niche. They are wellness oriented with an aversion to industrialization. If you have a product or service they can benefit from, you have found a good marketplace.

WHY PEOPLE BUY OR SEEK SERVICES

Internal Forces

Learning

The information consumers accumulate is remembered and reflected with each new experience. There is not only an individual accumulation but a social heritage. Look at the varied foods bought by people of different cultures. Most American do not lust after snails, or bird's nest soup, but their French or Chinese neighbors may. As people learn about products and services in their general sphere of contact, they develop buying habits. If they then move to another location, they must begin anew. At first, they seek out familiar stores that may be national or internationally positioned and try to find the old products they were in the habit of buying. Lacking these, they begin to replace items they can't locate with new ones and create new buying habits. (A good niche market for mental health professionals is providing services to those who are newly relocated. This is a time of severe stress and confusion.)

Perception

An individual's subjective perception is often more powerful than objective reality. For example, when people are asked to rate soft drinks, they generally top-rate their preferred brand. When given samples in a blindfold test, they often choose a different brand solely based on taste. Businesses use trademarks, logos, and celebrity endorsements to influence consumers' perceptions of their product or service. Professionals need to understand how they are perceived by the public and make honest changes if that perception is negative or confusing.

Personality

The diversity of personality measures makes it difficult to link personality attributes to consumption. The VALS instrument is an attempt to link personality characteristics to buying styles. Consider the ads for Jeeps and luxury cars. Generally, the Jeep ads feature a rugged individualist who is driving up a mountain or through a jungle. The luxury car ads are designed to attract persons who want to identify with material comforts and a quiet interior. Consider the type of personality you work best with. This will help you create your marketing pieces with the kind of language and images that will attract suitable clients.

Attitudes and Preferences

For the purposes of this book, an attitude means a learned predisposition to react in particular ways. A preference is the condition of liking Item A more than Item B. An individual may have learned to react cautiously when a telemarketer tries to sell him or her insurance. Or, a consumer, when deciding which type of insurance to buy, may prefer a local insurance broker rather than a national company with no representative in their hometown. The attitudes toward mental illness are always a problem in the general public. When mental health professionals market services, they are best served to identify the benefits the public will receive rather than the mental illnesses they treat.

Motivation

Maslow's hierarchy of needs comes into play in this area. You can assign goods and services to each level of development and predict how the consumer will respond. A man who is losing his job and home probably will not respond to joining a consciousness raising group. That person's focus is on safety and survival, not on perceived nonessentials. Consumers also tie in their spending to their perception of their standard of living. A family of five that is saving to put children through college is unlikely to choose the same automobile as the one owned by a single person with a large discretionary spending budget. Consumers can be internally or externally motivated. Think about the keeping-up-with-the-Joneses mentality as outer-driven motivation and seeking peace of mind as inner-driven motivation. After defining your ideal client, consider that individual's life motivators. Ask yourself how you can frame your outreach efforts to let such persons know you have what they want.

External Forces

Cultural Forces

Culture is a compilation of individual learning, history, values, morals, customs, art, and habits. These forces change and adapt to the environment. Within a major culture, there are also subcultures. Think of the United States as a large culture and Northerners or Southerners as social subcultures. There are other life-cycle cultures such as teenagers, yuppies, and the elderly, each with their own value system and needs. A family has its own life cycle and culture. Cultures are often stereotyped. It is important to look beyond culture to the individual. Ask yourself what cultural forces are at play in your ideal client's life.

Mobility

This refers to the changes in residence; socioeconomic changes; and educational, political, and lifestyle changes. The more mobile an individual is, the higher a risk taker he or she may be and the more willing to experiment with new products and services. If you are offering new ideas in the marketplace, mobile clients may be more inclined to try your offerings.

Lifestyle

Consider the different products a college student would buy compared with the preferences of a business executive. The first difference might be the kind of clothing they would choose. Students would likely seek out styles shown on television, in films, and in youth-oriented magazines. Business executives would consider their corporate culture and the cut of "power suit" currently in vogue. Your ideal client has a particular lifestyle including images and patterns of speech. Use these when communicating your services so readers will feel aligned with you.

Social Forces

Social forces are often broken into three major categories: group influence, personal influence, and interpersonal interaction. Your reference groups might include your profession, neighborhood, intimate partner(s), or your children. If you want to do a quick check on how society influences you, look at your major purchases or clothing styles and think about how your social arena determines your choices. What social forces affect your ideal client?

Personal Influence

This refers to the influence exerted by a significant other or by other professionals of the community. Since many human service practitioners do not advertise or talk about others in their field, consumers often have to take the advice of friends or trusted members of allied professions. If they need a psychotherapist, they might ask their physician, clergyperson, or a friend who has used such services. This word-of-mouth marketing is very valuable to mental health professionals.

Point-of-Contact Interaction Influence

This addresses the interaction between the consumer and the seller. A purchasing outcome is the result of information that is comfortable and convincing. A consumer who feels put off or distrusting of the interaction, will probably wait to buy until the interaction is more positive. It is important to have your initial telephone contact scripted so you ask the kinds of questions your ideal client feels comfortable with.

Economic Forces

Generally as people make more money, they spend more money. If they have a high credit line, they will rise to meet the limit. There is not a direct correlation between discretionary income and how much consumers spend, but there is a general trend. There is also the satiation effect. If people can buy a lot of one product, they will begin to devalue it. Consider children in a candy store. If they can go there any time and buy whatever kind of candy in any quantity they want, the magic will diminish and become instead a sugar addiction that will maintain the buying. Look to the marketplace and see if others are offering the same services you are providing. If there are, consider another geographic location or a new way of framing your work.

Marketing Forces

"Sale, today only," and "Now that you have purchased the basic unit, please consider our add-on products" are only two of the many marketing ploys we encounter daily. The printed media flood us with marketing approaches. Television bombards us with ads. The sign at the movie theater even pressures us to buy popcorn and soda: "Be sure to visit our snack bar before the movie begins." It is the marketer's job to persuade the consumer to buy. This is probably the biggest problem for ethical professionals. Their job is to make a match between consumers' needs and their service or product. The American culture is becoming increasingly marketing savvy and suspicious. This attitude makes it difficult to market honestly and sidestep the perception of undue persuasion. Authentic marketing helps you come across as genuine in your desire to offer your services to those who can honestly use them.

The Buying Process

There are individual styles and there are also some general buying processes, as described in the following sections.

Prepurchase Phase

This phase may last a long time or be a quick decision. First there comes the recognition of a need, then the search for ways to fill it. That could be easy, such as buying a product to replace a broken one. Making a decision about what to buy can be more difficult when a consumer enters a new marketplace and has no choice criteria. We have different criteria for different categories of products. This is reflected in a study in *Consumer Behavior* (Robertson, Zielinski, & Ward, 1984) showing that consumers buy bakery products on impulse 70 percent of the time and clothing on impulse only 24 percent of the time. Cookies are an impulse buy, and a new jacket is a more seriously deliberated purchase. When considering using mental health services, consumers often do not have selection criteria. Some professionals offer information on choosing a therapist. Others suggest they interview two or three people before making a choice. Many consumers simply wait until there is a crisis, and then they seek referrals to the most readily available provider. Yet, consumers who have made a thoughtful selection of a professional are more likely to continue to use their services.

Purchase Risk

There is often a degree of risk in buying a new product or service. The only risk in replacing a known item would be the discovery of a new or previously undetected defect. The risk of buying an unfamiliar product or service is much greater and probably will entail more serious consideration: Buying a pair of jeans of an unknown brand without trying them on is riskier than buying a set of sheets from a new manufacturer. Consumers who have been in therapy before will have some idea of what they want, and the risk will be lower.

Decision Maker

This is the person making the final decision to purchase (e.g., the mother of a family may be the decision maker for new household items, food items, and children's clothing; the father may make decisions about tools or automobiles). Children and teens have gained great purchasing capability, and are the targets of many companies' advertising. Watch Saturday morning cartoons if you're not convinced. The decision maker for mental health services for children is often their mother. The decision maker for couples varies. When the decision to obtain mental health services for a person has been made by somebody else, treatment motivation is generally low.

Purchasing Strategies

Individuals and groups develop particular purchasing behaviors. Consider:

- Some people will only buy clothing when there is a sale.
- Buyers who like to negotiate for price may not buy if the seller won't haggle with them.
- Women usually spend more time in supermarkets than men.
- Thursday, Friday, and Saturday are the busiest shopping days in most stores.

Families also develop habits around repeated purchases such as preferring a certain brand of peanut butter or type of bread. These strategies can be challenged through marketing efforts and often change will occur. On the other hand, familial purchasing habits have a strong effect on members, who may then describe these preferences to others who express interest. Mental health consumers may have difficulty accessing such information because of the stigma regarding mental illness. They may not be able to ask friends or family members for recommendations.

The Postpurchase Phase

Most people do not think about the postpurchase phase although it determines whether the customer returns. After the purchase, three critical factors come into play: satisfaction, loyalty, and dissonance.

Satisfaction

Did the purchase meet the needs of the consumer? There is the immediate feedback and more longitudinal feedback. Long-term feedback can be difficult to maintain. This is often the case with counseling. The problem may get worse before it gets better. It is the job of the therapist to predict this possibility while holding the long-term gain as a possibility.

Loyalty

This refers to repeat purchases. This commitment to a product or service can persist for years and be difficult to understand. You may buy the same laundry soap your grandmother used, without having compared it with newer products on the market. It could be the smell, the familiar box design, or the pleasant memory of helping her do the laundry that occurs every time you pick up the box. Family loyalty may prevent individuals from finding the products or services they need.

Dissonance

A temporary imbalance of the mind may occur after a purchase until the consumer integrates that purchase into the identity of self. When a consumer purchases a service or product that is incongruous with cognition, it may create a conflict with self-image, lifestyle, socioeconomic status, or loyalty to another product. If the purchase is highly satisfying, the dissonance disappears more quickly than if there is low satisfaction.

The stages of postpurchase dissonance are as follows:

- Rationalization.
- Accommodation.
- Rejection or acceptance.
- Resolution.

Practitioners who provide mental health services should be sensitive to dissonance and help their clients reframe and accommodate the seeking of such services into their sense of self.

MARKET RESEARCH

Marketing research is one of the most important tasks to ensure success and yet is the least practiced activity of the human services professional. Whereas it may seem manipulative to figure out your client, this quest can be reframed to mean identifying how your marketing can most effectively reach the person who needs your services. Market research simply seeks to learn the composition of the marketplace and whether a particular service or product can serve its needs. Market research is not a one-time event but should be constant.

Mental health services professionals could use a questionnaire for each client who leaves the practice or do a needs assessment of a particular group. Market research should evaluate the environment and the consumer.

Information Goals

Decide:

- What do you want to know about the marketplace and your ideal client?
- How are you going to gather that information?
- What are you going to do with it?

Here are some general guidelines for how *not* to do research:

- Never begin your research before defining your business and research purpose and objectives.
- Don't start your research without a budget.
- Avoid wording your questions to get desired responses.
- Don't forget to follow up nonresponders to your outreach.
- Don't let someone else decide what you want to know.
- Be careful not to use just the portion of your research that validates your expectations.

Tools and Techniques in Marketing Research

First and foremost in the art of gathering information is walking around and asking questions. You have probably been accosted by someone in a shopping mall who wanted you to stop in your tracks and proffer some information. Most people don't want to take the time, but when a friend or colleague asks the questions, most of us are willing to give our opinion. Most human service professionals enjoy talking to people so this work should be enjoyable. Your market research can be as informal or structured as you choose as long as you get the information you need to succeed.

Regional Assessments

Whenever you have or plan to have a business in a particular geographic area, it is always a good idea to get some basic information. When I started my first practice, I simply decided to have it close to home so I could throw the keys to my car in the basket by the door and leave them there. Looking back, this was not the best decision-making system to choose the right location. Luckily, my area was not already saturated by professionals. When I decided to relocate my counseling practice in a large city, I used the same system but had poorer results. Most cities are saturated with mental health professionals making it more difficult to start a new business. When I changed the focus of my business from psychotherapy to practice consultation, I no longer had that problem. With both decisions, however, I should have undertaken several regional assessments before making an emotional commitment and financial outlay. The following sections describe the critical factors for investigation.

Saturation

How many professionals are in your desired area? I suggest you get a map and a compass and draw a circle around the area that allows for the density of the population. A high-density area would have a smaller circle and a low-density area a larger circle. Now you know the area where you will gather information for your assessment. Contact professionals in this region to find out the following information:

Market Fees

- What do they charge?
- Do they use a sliding scale?
- Are they doing business with managed care companies?

Some professionals will be willing to talk to you about their practice and some will be reticent. When I moved to a new area, I got out the telephone book and made a list of everybody with a mental health practice. I called them all and said I was new to the area and wanted to get a sense of the professional community. Some never returned my phone calls, and others were willing to meet me for lunch. Don't take it personally if respondents put you off, and cherish those who will share their time and information with you.

Some professionals will tell you what companies they are doing business with and others won't. These attitudes represent the abundance and the deficit mentalities. The deficit mentality believes that if you know who their clients are, you will scoop them out of the way and take away business. The abundance mentality believes the opposite: If I tell you who has requested my services and it is a good match for you, then we can swap referrals when our areas of expertise do not match the needs of the client. I have always found the abundance mentality serves me better than the deficit. Other people somehow will find out what you didn't want to tell them. If you have been helpful, you will have a friend, colleague, or potential referral resource. If you have not been helpful, you have no relationship and possibly an enemy. I prefer the former.

Licenses, Certifications, Credentials. Find out what kinds of licenses, certifications, and credentials your state offers in your area of expertise. What type of license do you have? Is it covered by a practice law or a title law? If it is a practice law, other people cannot say they provide the kind of services you are licensed to offer. If it is a title law, they only need to call themselves something other than the license title. They can advertise the same services as you as long as they are not misrepresenting themselves as having skills they do not hold. Gather data on the following questions:

- How many professionals hold the same license or certification that you have?
- How many are in your region?

- How many are close to your office?
- How many people are providing the kind of services or specialties you do?
- What other kinds of professionals might be referral sources?

Use of Alternative Medicines. What forms of alternative or related services are in your region? A substantial portion of the healthcare dollar is being spent out of pocket for alternative or complementary services such as massage, herbology, and acupuncture. Often these practitioners would like to know and work with professionals who are willing to talk about how their approaches overlap and complement one another. A healthy referral system can come out of such collaborations.

Product and Service Development

Positioning

Most mental health professionals are familiar with the terms *framework* and *reframing.* A framework provides a context or structure around which a behavior, thought, or feeling exists. The *reframe* is made when a change is desired and the perspective is altered. A good example is a group watching two cars running into each other head-on. If this occurs at a demolition derby, the audience is excited and generally not too concerned about anyone getting hurt since careful safety measures usually protect the drivers. If the collision takes place at a busy intersection, the observers' reaction will be very different. Thus, the power of the framework.

All perspectives are valid, although they vary greatly. If you want to know someone's context or viewing position, you need to reframe what you see. What does this have to do with positioning yourself in the marketplace? The marketplace is the framework and your position is how you are perceived within that context. Think of the difference in how you are positioned if you have an office in an upscale professional area or provide direct services at homeless shelters. You might do both well. But you would need to let those people who see you from one perspective know about the other perspective since they may never consider it as an option.

It is up to you to take some responsibility for your public perception. Consumers will make decisions about you with or without your help. It is in your best interest to help them understand where you stand and how they should perceive you. Keep in mind that consumer behavior is not static; it changes from year to year as people react to new trends and events. No longer can professionals trust that what they are currently doing will continue to be valued by people for any predictable time.

Your marketing approach needs to be collaborative. You need to match the providers' perceptions and resources, and the individual's or group's needs, with the service or products of your profession. All mental health professionals must be aware of their public perception, and then position themselves in a way that best communicates who they are. I consider it a moral imperative for your local community to know what skills you can offer so they can use them in time of need. The exercise shown in Figure 4.2, "The Story of Your Success," can help you identify your strengths, weaknesses, opportunities, and threats. This SWOT analysis can give you a good sense of your current position in the marketplace.

Figure 4.2

The Story of Your Success

You can create this story in writing or speak it into a tape recorder. I suggest you do both. It is one thing to read a story; it is another to hear it. Organize your story with the following captions:

The History of Your Work in the Profession

When did you start doing this kind of work (it may have been as a small child playing office)?

How has it evolved? Include your education and other experiences that involved your professional learning.

Your Philosophy about the Profession

How do you see your profession fitting into the overall culture or business marketplace?

What is your personal philosophy about its importance?

(Continued)

Figure 4.2 *(Continued)*

Your Personal Treatment Methodology

How do you help people grow and change?

What products do you find most helpful?

The Objectives You Have for Your Future

These are your goals. Try to describe them as concretely as possible. They must be SMART: **S**pecific, **M**easurable, **A**ccessible, **R**ealistic, and **T**imely.

Your Professional Strengths

What can you do particularly well?

What do others notice you excel at?

(Continued)

Figure 4.2 *(Continued)*

Your Professional Weakness

What do you believe you could be better at?

Is there any training you believe you need to stay current in your field?

What resources are limited and holding you back?

Any Problems or Threats You Are Facing at This Time

These are problems that relate to your professional success. They may be personal in nature, as well as business related.

Professional Opportunities

What opportunities are currently on the horizon?

(Continued)

Figure 4.2 *(Continued)*

Turning Bugs into Features

Analyze your problem(s) and plans for the future. Turn bugs into features. How can you change your problems into opportunities? Continue planning your successful future.

Conclusion or Summary

Include all of the above in your SWOT analysis.

Positioning Attributes

What other qualities contribute to your market position? Here are some factors to think about:

- *Pricing.* What you charge says a lot about your value system and lifestyle. If you are charging at the top or over the marketplace, you are in a different position from that of the professional who uses a sliding scale or pro bono in his or her practice. There is value to both positions. The individual with the highest fees is usually automatically considered the best in that arena, whatever the truth may be. The person at the other end of the scale is considered more humanistic and possibly self-sacrificing. Consider the position your ideal client would prefer.
- *Individual Definition.* How do you define yourself? Factors like the following ones identify your image:

  The clothes you wear. Is it a Brooks Brothers suit or skirt and blouse or jeans and a comfortable jacket?

  The car you drive. Is it a well-worn Volkswagen Beetle, or a new Cadillac or BMW?

These things may not seem important to you, but they are to your clients. At least have an awareness of what they see about you.

Products and Services

Distribution and Logistics

Do you have one office or offer services at many locations? Are you the community-identified professional in your area or are you nationally known for your expertise? Local professionals are easier to approach than national celebrities. Fame may do many things for your ego, but it won't necessarily contribute to your pocketbook unless you leverage it. If you have recently become well known and respected because of some event or publication, use that image now to your best advantage through other contracts, speaking engagement, or product endorsements.

Marketing Communications

Marketing communications include how you position and then communicate your product or services. Your product or service is the sum of the physical and psychological satisfaction consumers receive when they purchase. This is called the total offering of the product or service and all the other pieces of the marketing mix.

Product or Service

This refers to the core product or actual benefit or service derived from the product. It determines what consumers can sense, feel, and think about your offering and includes things like packaging, logo, and special features.

Line

A group of closely related products or services that satisfy a class of needs, are used together, or fall within the same price range is known as a *line.* An example is a professional who offers hypnosis and sells her own hypnosis book and audiotapes, and offers hypnosis training seminars.

Mix

A business may offer a composite list of products for sale. Such offerings are called a *mix.*

Width

This refers to the extent of the producer's or professional's market. Using the example of the hypnotist, consider how wide the market may be for her training seminars. She might train licensed professionals, certified mental health workers, and the community in the skill of self-hypnosis.

Depth

An individual's or company's depth refers to the average number of product items or services offered by the individual or company within each product line. Our hypnotist offers individual hypnosis sessions, a hypnosis book, hypnosis audiotapes, hypnosis training videotapes, a community television program, and has a home page on the Internet.

Number of Product Lines within a Company

Our hypnotist may also offer sports medicine consultation. Be careful not to dilute your core product services with too many alternative products or services. Most people know you cannot be all things to all people. It is in your best interest to follow what you are good at and keep your product width within a reasonable range. Also, there must be that thread of continuity between your products and services. Our hypnotist might also be a good surfer and want to offer classes at the beach. Unless she connects the two services, (e.g., how hypnosis can enhance sports performance), the public will begin to have cognitive dissonance about who she is. To avoid internal conflict, they will no longer consider her a valid option for any of her services or products.

MARKET DEVELOPMENT

As Ms. Hypnotist networks, practices her craft, and stays abreast of her field, she may see new ways to apply her craft to benefit others. As she identifies new opportunities, she needs to do her homework (market research) before she goes to market. If Ms. Hypnotist has a stream of new products and services coming and going in the marketplace, she will dilute her identity and lose customers. The various offerings need to be developed behind the curtain of research and development. When she is certain she has developed an offering she feels good about and is qualified to offer, then, and only then, should she bring it to the public.

Increasing the Market

The hypnotist can increase her market by adding or changing attributes to her offerings. The following can be altered to make her offering a "new" item:

- New cost, higher or lower.
- New convenience in use or access.
- New performance.
- New availability—more classes, hours, or locations.

Decreasing the Market

The market is sensitive to change. The following are ways to decrease the demand for services or products:

- *New Methods of Use.* People will avoid methods that are new and are not noticeably easier.

- *Unfamiliar Patterns of Use.* An example is a way to use hypnosis to teach your cat to brush its teeth. This service is not something the average cat owner will take on easily.
- *Unfamiliar Benefit.* People who don't know they need something, can be suspicious of you for imposing a benefit that implies a previously unfelt need. Be careful to frame benefits in terms most consumers will recognize.

Market Lifecycle

If you follow the history of mental illness in the United States and the identity of mental health professionals, you can see great change. Mental health professionals started as the jailers of the prisons and evolved into the doctors who ran the mental institutions. These institutions changed into regional treatment centers. After Freud made his mark in America, mental health professionals were perceived as his followers. Mental health professionals have gradually changed into a league of different professions and approaches. These professionals can now be found in hospitals, agencies, or the private sector. Many professionals do not believe that this will change. Others predict that the mental health profession will merge into one identity. No longer will there be psychiatrists, psychologists, social workers, marriage counselors, professional counselors, substance abuse specialists, and more; the blanket term *mental health professional* will be used instead.

You need to know your profession's history and the trends regarding change. The marketplace is changing much more rapidly now than it did 50 years ago. I don't believe professionals will be able to continue offering the same services for many years, as they have done in the past. They will need to constantly match their expertise with the needs and perceptions of the marketplace.

The Marketing River and Its Tributaries

How do products and services get to their end user? The marketing river is the path or journey they take from the service provider or product manufacturer. Think of the journey an office visit takes in the managed care river:

1. The client or consumer signs up at work with a health carrier.
2. The mental health coverage is contracted out to a carve-out provider.
3. The mental health carve-out provider has a panel of providers in the consumer's geographic area with different specialties.
4. The consumer or potential client makes a call to the health carrier and describes his or her problem.
5. The health carrier refers the client to the carve-out mental health system.
6. This provider system directs the person to a case manager who gives a referral.
7. The employee calls the provider and makes an appointment.
8. The provider then must call the mental health carve-out to verify coverage before seeing the new client.
9. Once the new client is seen, he or she must be diagnosed and that diagnosis must be verified for coverage by the carve-out mental health system.

10. The client is finally provided with the needed services.

Consider the many variables in this single scenario. Possibly the health carrier publishes a directory of providers and leaves it up to the client to locate a provider. Maybe the client has to see one professional to do an assessment who then refers the person to another long-term provider. And so it goes. It is important to become aware of how your offerings are accessed. You need to retain as much control as possible over how you are presented or represented so you can maintain your market position. It is essential to be in close alignment with as many channels of delivery as possible. If you value quality in your services, you do not want to be in relationship with a company, referral service, or other access arena that does not follow the same standards you do. Remember, every piece of the marketing mix has an impact on your client. Keep it as high quality and congruent as you possibly can. The fewer people or businesses between you and the consumer, the truer your identity will remain; the more there are, the higher the likelihood your identity will be diluted. Be cooperative with those who are part of your river, and do your best to find a common language between yourself and those who represent you. Their success, is your success, so don't undermine their efforts.

Making a Marketing Match Using Ethical Standards

Now is the time to consider who you are in the professional sense and who your ideal client is. Once this is done, you can honestly begin to find one another. The old song, "The Boxes," by Simon and Garfunkel, has the lyric, "A man hears what he wants to hear and disregards the rest." This is generally true in marketing and communication. If you don't speak the same language as your clients, they will not hear you. Many professionals have a glass tower mentality. They sit in their office with their clients daily, socialize with professionals in their arena, and cease to understand other perspectives. When these professionals go out and create marketing pieces, they wonder why clients don't come flocking to their doors. Essentially, their brochures were written by aliens from a different planet. That is the way you need to think of the clients who will be coming to you. They are aliens who live on another planet, and you need to figure out how to let them know you have what they are looking for, and why they would best be served by coming to you.

Marketing as a Way of Life

Have you ever heard the comment that marketing is just a numbers game? That is one approach. There are statistics in the telemarketing game about how many phone calls you have to make to get one lead. As you can probably guess, the numbers are high. Most professionals are not attracted to this type of marketing. I also believe it is a short-term solution and most professionals are in for the long run. The long-term solution is to develop a good product or service and expand it over the years. You build personal integrity, client loyalty, and a set of networks that will support you through hard times. With this solution, marketing becomes a way of life.

Marketing Should Be a Way of Life with a Budget Attached to It

Some people think that the successful marketer has hit upon some kind of magic or luck. Usually, a good marketing plan is what supports their success. You need a working marketing plan that can change with you. Planning helps you organize and facilitates clear thinking about your marketing activities. You will check the logic and expense behind each move, while considering alternate plans. It also helps you coordinate your actions and allows you to leverage off other events to your best advantage.

There Must Be Another Way

Recently, I was sitting in a meeting with many people I did not know. We were planning a new approach to get into a corporate market. One of the members said, "What we need are some marketing people." When I asked her why she had said that, she replied, "I don't know anything about marketing." When I next inquired whether she could describe her ideal client, she paused and admitted that she had never thought about it. To my final question, "How will your marketing people know how to sell your services if they don't know which market to target?" her reply was simple: "That's their problem." She was confident that the marketing person would just know it.

Not wanting to push the matter any further in the group, I bit my tongue while my mind raced to the consequences of that approach. So many therapists hand off the most important aspect of their professional growth to someone else—to a marketer who doesn't care whether they stay and flourish in their counseling profession. The marketer may not understand the work therapists do, may not believe in its importance, may not understand the needs of potential clients, and will only promote the services when the payment clock is ticking. It is in the best interest of all professionals to do their homework before engaging in any consultative relationship; ideally, they should do their own marketing.

Marketing Support Groups

Marketing is usually the last thing mental health professionals put on their list of things to do. To turn this habit around, try to create or join a marketing support group made up of professionals who have an interest in growing their practice (they do not need to be in the same business as your own practice). A diverse group can be a rich source of new ideas and referrals. Meet frequently, so you don't lose your momentum. When you think of marketing efforts you are still afraid of, partner up with someone who will go with you or may have done it before.

I also suggest keeping a marketing journal. I save copies of every marketing piece I have ever created. It is helpful to go back over the years and see how my offerings have evolved. It also helps me keep a thread of continuity in my marketing efforts so that the client who worked with me 10 years ago will still know who I am today and can see how I have developed my present practice.

5

DEVELOPING A MARKETING PLAN

Marketing Phobia

Do you print business cards, brochures, or fliers and keep them in your drawer? Have you ever attended a networking event and reduced your anxiety with frequent trips to the food table or the bathroom? Because I have lived these experiences and often have listened to clients as they described the same feelings, I have identified a new clinical syndrome specific to mental health professionals: *marketing phobia.* Marketing phobia may be organic or learned. Consider our backgrounds. Mental health professionals receive training to take care of others' needs, work in an industry that discourages dual relationships, and offer services that carry a social stigma (mental illness). We offer services that, if used, identify the user as socially suspicious (mentally ill). We can't tell people they need our services if we notice a problem (diagnosis in public); we can't offer services to satisfied clients' family or friends (dual relationships); and we have to be scrupulously honest in all our marketing efforts (ethical standards). Mental health professionals have the makings of a real marketing challenge. Unlike others who sell products and services, you cannot offer guaranteed quick cures, reduced rates for frequent fliers, or speak about your latest success story in great detail.

My decision to go public with this marketing phobia came from a poignant meeting with a mental health professional. She came to me because she had become disturbed that she was not getting as many referrals as she used to from colleagues, and her practice was slowly dying. As she told me how she had practiced successfully for years without telling anybody about what she did, I wondered if I was hearing her correctly. Her conviction that things should continue as before prompted her to proudly show me her business card with her name, address, and telephone number on it. There was no mention of degree, license, or specialty; she could have been a bookkeeper. She confirmed my impression that she was deliberately hiding from the public and intended to continue to do so.

I have heard this story so often, I knew I had to share with others how deeply embedded this syndrome is in our profession. You are not alone.

If mental health is to flourish, mental health professionals need to realize that there are ethical ways of marketing their services and then they must learn those techniques. Help yourself while you help others and stand up to be counted: Break the bonds of marketing phobia.

REFRAME OF MARKETING

When people ask me what I do and I reply I'm in marketing, the response is usually ambiguous. They are fascinated with the idea of marketing, but generally think of marketing as something people do to try to manipulate others. A common belief is that marketers are not to be trusted. Everyone is familiar with the image of the fast-talking used car salesperson, who may not always tell the truth. This image doesn't have to apply to you.

I was terrified when I first started marketing. I was selling products I had created with my own hands, and if someone didn't like them, I felt as if the person had rejected me. I watched a friend sell my creative items with ease. He had no problem proclaiming their beauty. I wanted to be able to do the same. The problem was that I was not sure of the value of the art items I had created. My attitude has changed: Now I feel very good about the services I offer and have no problem telling others about their value. I have come to identify this kind of marketing as *authentic marketing:* the authentic marketing of the self by the self. The key ingredient is feeling competent and good about what you have to offer.

Authentic marketing is what you do naturally when you know who you are and where you want to be in the future. Promoting your work allows you to show your "inner integrity and crystallized sense of self" (Huang & Lynch, 1992). Marketing or selling that is designed to conquer consumers' buying habits, creates a counterwave of determination in consumers to follow their own direction. An alternative to manipulative aggressive marketing approaches is the concept of following the Tao. The Tao refers to the process of being connected to the limitless power of the universe and acting in accordance with the forces of nature by aligning yourself with the natural flow of energy or events (Huang & Lynch, 1992). There is no forcing or imposing of your expression; you simply allow it to follow its own natural path of least resistance.

Think of two boats on a rushing river. One has a gas engine and the captain navigates the waters carefully to hold to what he believes is the best course. The second boat is a light but sturdy craft that is well balanced and built specifically for its course. When placed in the river, it flows with the rushing water, bumping off logs, and rocks, and dancing on the waves. Which boat will travel faster? Most people think it will be the second boat, but believe it may crash and sink to the bottom—that it doesn't is the point. If the vessel is strong, sturdy, and well designed for the course of the river, it will reach its destination quickly. If its structure was poorly conceived, and its path was chosen after construction, users of that boat should be cautious about trusting its performance. Albert Einstein described the experience of acting in harmony with life:

> Life takes the form of a rapturous amazement at the harmony of natural law, which reveals an intelligence of such superiority (wholeness) that, compared with it, all systematic thinking and acting of human beings is utterly insignificant. (Boldt, 1993)

An effective self-marketer's assertiveness comes from constantly fine-tuning the expression of self-works and seeking the arenas in which there is a natural atunement or dynamic movement. In marketing terms, this is *finding your niche.* By constantly refining your service or product and persistently navigating the marketing river, success comes quickly, and there is great joy in the journey. This may seem like a naive and idealistic idea in today's business culture, often likened to swimming with sharks. Keep in mind how much energy people must use when they are not connected to what they do. Imposing needs and manipulating others may be more successful in the short run, but it is less successful in the long run. Resources are depleted more quickly, and you cannot optimize the product or service. You must be in this for the long run. If you aren't, don't use the ideas in this book; they are designed for long-term success.

From Competition to Collegiality

Think of two sets of tennis players. One set plays to dominate and defeat their opponent. They are outer directed. The other set of players focus on personal performance and constantly make changes to optimize that performance. They are inner directed. At the conclusion of the first players' game, someone wins and the other loses. They may have learned something, but it is framed from the perspective of reacting to an outside stimulus, outer directed. The other set of players performs from the perspective of constantly improving their performance. This match has a win-win outcome. Both players have improved their game and have each other to thank for the challenges they faced.

Collaboration

I was talking to a friend recently who had decided to keep secret—not to share—(she thought) information about some business resources. The colleague whose request she refused found another way to get that information. My friend now had someone who wouldn't share with her, and nothing had been gained. In today's information culture, there are so many new ways to access information, it is difficult to keep anything secret. It is in everyone's best interest to share what they know and partner with others to expand their knowledge. As Martin Luther King, Jr., said:

> It really boils down to this: that all life is interrelated. We are all caught in an inescapable network of mutuality, tied into a single garment of density. Whatever affects one directly, affects all indirectly. (Boldt, 1993)

AUTHENTIC MARKETING

Human service professionals often have difficulty marketing their work because it sits so close to home. When—with my help—they identify the work they believe they are called to do and learn to language and market that service or product, there is no stopping them. This *authentic marketing process* derives from the professional who is following his or her heart and involves the consumer. When professionals offer something they truly believe the consumer needs, it is considered an authentic need.

Fundamental Tenets of Authentic Marketing

Not only the Puritans, but Freud and many others have taught that work represents a primary purpose in life. In today's American culture, some kind of work is an integral part of a balanced life. In the ideal sense, work is a personal expression of your talents and skills. Consequently, the presentation of your work is linked to your sense of self and self-esteem. When you believe in what you are doing you can apply yourself to it wholeheartedly. The Eastern concept of dharma means *right work.* When you do not do the kind of work that naturally expresses who you are, it whittles away at your personal integrity. Just as the concept of work needs to be reframed, so does the marketing of work.

Authentic Marketing as a Moral Imperative

It is your responsibility to communicate what you have to offer from your education and experience, in a way that can be accessed by those who need your expertise. If you were a heart specialist in a theater where someone had a heart attack and did not come forward to help, would that be a good moral decision? Similarly, if you know how to help families live together in peace and don't let your community know you are available, they will lose a valuable resource.

Client-Centered Collaborative Marketing

The task now becomes bringing your products or services to those who need them. You can educate others about how to use what you offer by entering into a dialogue with customers, not by imposing needs or values. The interaction is collaborative, not forceful. You use the skills you have developed as a clinician and try to understand people's needs. Then, you present your offerings to interested customers, and explain how they can benefit from your services.

Like the maker of baskets in the marketplace, you must develop relationships with new customers. They may have some ideas about how your services could be more useful to them in ways you had never thought of. They can help you learn your ideal client's language and show you new ways of seeing your services and products.

Helping People Understand Their Needs

If you are offering something new, it is your responsibility to learn how to communicate what you offer and how it can benefit others. Don't expect others to understand intuitively what you are talking about. Some may, but more won't. If you think of your new customers as aliens from another planet, as mentioned earlier, you will recognize that you must help them understand your offerings and provide everything they need to enter your world. Creators of a new concept or product often understand it so deeply that they forget many elements may be obscure to others. Thus, the alien concept. Always assume you need to explain everything in detail and be pleasantly surprised when you interact with someone who thinks the way you do, and understands quickly what you are presenting.

The Six Stages of Marketing Development

The six stages of marketing development parallel the development of the professional. As you evolve as a professional, you will develop a sense of who you are, and what you are doing, and will become confident about your work. When you understand what stage you are moving through, you can emphasize your strengths. The stages are:

1. Identifying the professional self.
2. Naming your chosen treatment methodologies, diagnoses, and models.
3. Creating your own paradigm.
4. Evolving your paradigm to another beginning.
5. Transitioning into a new arena.
6. Reidentifying the professional self.

Identifying the Professional Self

In this stage, professionals generally pass their licensing or certification process or secure a job with new professional responsibilities. While you have earned the right to offer your services, you will not want to present yourself as a seasoned professional because you are new to the field. You may feel more comfortable if you partner up with a colleague who has been in the business longer. Many companies sell very good training packages that include a trainer's manual, customer or client materials, props, and even marketing materials. Some professionals work for years in the field and obtain their licensure or certification after many years of experience. If you belong to this group, you will probably progress quickly through this stage and move ahead. You may feel a little different with your new labels after your name. Say them repeatedly, so you will feel comfortable when you go out and market yourself. Say them alone, to family, friends, and strangers in the supermarket. The key is practice.

Naming Your Chosen Treatment Methodologies, Diagnoses, and Models

During this stage, many professionals find a treatment methodology they resonate with strongly. It validates their personal experience and just makes sense to them. At this stage, you feel comfortable naming yourself as an expert in your chosen specialty. This identity can be a particular method of psychotherapy (Gestalt, psychodynamic, feminist) or be a particular diagnosis you work well with (eating disorders, depression, families). When you move out of the psychotherapy business into a training, consulting, or other role, this can be your new area of specialty. Whatever it is, you must feel confident about your skills or it will affect your marketing habits. You won't have the drive to promote yourself. If there is an arena you enjoy working in, I suggest you get the best training, supervision, mentoring, and experience you can. If you are thinking of branching out to managed care companies, many of them will ask for proof of training in any area you declare as a specialty.

Creating Your Own Paradigm

You have worked for many years and been exposed to many ideas. You have worked with a variety of people in different settings and have begun, or firmly created, your own treatment, training, or consulting methodology. If you haven't written it down, now is the time. Many professionals reach this stage. They have an internal understanding but never articulate it clearly to others. The process of articulation will be valuable in many ways. Although it can be a time-consuming task, writing down your experiences will make you really think about what you are doing. You may want to audio- or videotape your work. You may want to talk to a trusted colleague and practice explaining what you do. Tape this conversation as well. I don't know how many times I have heard myself telling someone else what I did and have thought, almost in surprise, *That sounds great.* The most obvious outcomes are publishing articles and writing your own book. The greatest obstacle to professionals at this point is misplaced self-consciousness: *What if people think I'm stupid?* If what you are doing is creating change and results, your ideas are not stupid. You may just not have worded your thoughts in a way that people can understand—keep at it and get a good editor. You have created a new way or resource. In Stage 3, let others know so they also can have that resource. Create a path that others can follow until they are ready to make their own.

Evolving Your Paradigm to Another Beginning

I find this to be one of the most exciting stages. After you have articulated what you do and have it firmly in mind, you will begin to see new arenas where you can apply it. The awareness is like that of a small child who discovers the Phillips screwdriver and then begins to notice all the places people have put those funny-looking screws, just asking to be turned. During this phase, it is even more important for you to network with people in other lines of work. As long as your new creation is a way of working with people, it can be applied anywhere they are. The world is your arena for exploring ways to apply your craft.

Transitioning into a New Arena (Go Back to Stage 1)

This is the arena that professionals have the most difficulty moving into. They have put so much time, money, and self-identity into creating who they are as professionals, they may have great difficulty taking on a new identity. I usually suggest they keep their old professional identity and just ask it to move over and make room for a new role. I have found it helpful to have different clothes for performing different roles. I have my therapist outfits, my trainer outfits, and my consulting wardrobe. As time goes on, they begin to merge into a single resource telling me I am integrating my roles into my personal identity. When I pick up a new role, I go to events frequented by those professionals and watch what they wear, listen to how they talk, and pick up other cues about their identifying culture. Then, I choose the elements I feel comfortable with and begin to take on the new role. This leads back to Stage 1.

Reidentifying the Professional Self

Around and around we go: In today's marketplace, you need to constantly evolve into the next stage of your professional development. Conscious evolution is highly superior to forced change. Choose how you are going to change rather than having it forced on you because you lose your job or your business declines.

GETTING READY TO MARKET

If you have been applying your craft, you have been marketing. You have been creating a personal presence and a position in the marketplace. You are ready to market right now, this instant. The next step is to see if you can describe who you are, what you do, why you do it, why others will benefit from what you do, and how they can get more involved with you.

Personal Marketing Formula

Practice the following formula by yourself. Start by writing down key words on 3-by-5-inch cards that trigger what you want to say. If you read a script, you will bore people and they won't listen to you. You can start by recording your spontaneous answers to the questions and drawing your key words from that text. The most important requirement is that you feel good about what you are saying. The second important requirement is that your new customer hears what is most important. When you can speak your message in less than three minutes, with ease, begin sharing it with trusted colleagues and people in other fields of work. When you are through, ask them what they heard. Did they hear what you wanted them to hear? Try to be unbiased. Maybe they are hearing something you need to be consciously saying. If it is going to come out of your presentation, even if you didn't plan it, maybe you should integrate it into your descriptions.

Who Are You?

This can include your license, certification, or role. What do you want your listeners to know about who you are, and where do you want to be positioned in the marketplace?

> *Example:* I am Susan Froid, a Licensed Clinical Social Worker with a private practice in Boston's financial center.

Don't you already have a mental image of Sue?

What Do You Do?

Frame your work in terms of benefits to your customers. At first, people are usually not interested in how you do it. Initially, they want to hear good news outcomes. "I do couples counseling" could be reframed "I help couples learn how to enjoy each other again." If you are having difficulty thinking of your work in terms of benefits, open the yellow pages and check under the heading your work would fall under. If you find none of them are framed as benefits, call the telephone company and order a book from the largest city near you. Usually yellow pages salespeople in large cities help their customers frame their business in terms of benefits.

> *Example:* I work with professional women and help them excel in their work and increase their quality of life. Often they need help overcoming learned helplessness, gaining assertiveness skills, and enhancing their self-presentation. More often, they need help with the stress of being a woman in a highly competitive marketplace trying to keep their home clean and comfortable, and finding time to create and maintain nurturing relationships.

Your image of Sue is expanding rapidly.

Why Do You Do It?

This is where the real sense of Sue will come forth. You will begin to understand why she does what she has told you about. You will learn a little about who she is personally. The most important thing is that you see where her passions lie, the force that keeps her constantly improving her work.

> *Example:* I had to enter the workplace when I was 16. I have had very good and very bad jobs and bosses. Being a single parent for many of those years, I look back and wonder how I survived and how my children grew up as healthy as they are. I never had any time. I went to school until I could become my own

> boss and take control of my life. Now I truly enjoy helping other women excel in their work, take control of their lives, and follow their dreams. Recently, I received a letter from a woman who came to me when her husband left her. She had been the bookkeeper in his business. She started her own bookkeeping business and continued to raise her two sons. She has been successful with both and wrote to tell me how well she is doing. When my clients send me letters like that, they bring tears to my eyes and remind me how important my work is.

Now what do you think of Sue? Is she someone you might consider as a resource? Is there anyone you know who might want to use her to solve some problems or learn new skills? In any case, you will remember what Sue does when you see her next time.

Why You Might Be Interested

Now that Sue has described what she does, Sue's audience needs to hear the benefits of working with her.

> *Example:* I find that when women's self-esteem increases, their new assertiveness helps them get the things out of life they always wanted. They are able to redefine their own sense of personal power and create their lives, rather than react to what life offers them.

How We Can Continue to Develop Our Relationship

Now is the time for Sue to tell the people she is networking with how to find her. She might hand them her card, tell them about a training program she is doing, invite them to an event they might be interested in, get them on her mailing list for upcoming events, or arrange to get together for lunch. If Sue is marketing her professional counseling services, she won't go to lunch, but may tell others about her informational sessions and what they cost. Sue by now has been listening to her contacts and has a sense of what their needs are. She should frame the *How* message to ease them to the next stage of the marketing process.

> *Example:* You might be interested in, or know other women who would like to come to one of my evening drop-in support groups for working women. I also have a newsletter that has tips to help women balance their lives. I have to admit I slip in healthy quick recipes when I find them. Here is my card in case you know a working woman who needs some help or support or might like my free newsletter. Do you have a card?

Wouldn't it be easy for just about anyone to receive her newsletter?

To summarize, the *Personal Marketing Formula* includes:

- Who you are.
- What you do.
- Why you do it.
- Why others might be interested in what you do (benefits).
- How the relationship can develop in the future.

You have completed the first step of a marketing plan. You have articulated a vision. Now you need to take the steps that will give substance to your dreams.

YOUR MARKETING PLAN

Why Create a Marketing Plan?

I have already described what marketing is. It includes everything you do that applies to your professional practice: your business cards, how you answer the phone, what kind of furniture and literature you have in your office. As you market authentically, with integrity, you begin to understand more deeply who and what you are and what you want for your future. For your marketing efforts to succeed, you must have a plan. A marketing plan can help in many ways:

- It forces you to evaluate your professional practice.
- It gives you a timetable with goals that you can refer to and evaluate during the year.
- It allows a consultant to look at what you are trying to accomplish and offer help.
- It gives you a sense of control and power over your future.

Standard Approaches

There are some standard approaches to beginning a marketing plan. Most marketing experts suggest that you explore the following questions:

- What business problems do you face?
- What are your goals?
- Who are your current client sources?
- Who are your competitors and what do they offer?
- What are the most successful ways you've promoted your business in the past?
- What promotional strategies have been the least effective and why?
- What is your USP (unique sales principle)? How are you different from others offering the same services?
- How do you know your services are needed?
- What other services can you offer that would be useful to the needs of the population you already serve?
- What additional training can make your services more marketable?
- Who are your target referral sources?
- What benefits can you offer this group?
- What promotional tactics will you use?
- What is your marketing budget?
- How will you measure return on your marketing dollar?
- List the things in your practice you would like to phase out?
- What do you most enjoy about your work?

These are all good things to think about. There is more to marketing and selling than thinking. There is a lot of emotion and even more of your personal style. I believe many professionals have difficulty marketing partly because they don't feel it is connected to what they do. That is why taking a personal approach to marketing and selling is critical for your success.

Self-Analysis

Start by identifying where you stand in your professional development and match that to your marketing developmental phase. You may already have found your current marketing materials don't match where you stand today. You may be behind or ahead of yourself. If that dissonance is working for you, fine. Usually it doesn't. People usually aren't as quick to distribute marketing pieces they don't feel completely comfortable with. This means you have to start working from where you are today and plan to develop to the next level. Your marketing efforts must have a thread of continuity. This can mean a logo, a graphic style, a color, or theme. When a person looks at today's marketing materials, they need to be able to recognize you in your future marketing pieces. To identify your professional strengths, complete the exercise in Figure 5.1. When you run out of answers, you have probably found the area you are working on. You can then decide how far you have come and choose to market from the previous stage because you feel comfortable with it. Or, you can jump to the next stage because you feel competent enough to work there.

Client Analysis

Now that you know what stage you are working out of, it is time to describe the ideal client or customer to whom you will offer your services. Use the following demographics to describe this client.

- Age.
- Sex.
- Income.
- Marital status.
- Size of household.
- Education.
- Geographical location.
- Special issues.
- Reading habits.
- Profession(s).
- Presenting problem.

Now review the attributes of your ideal client. If individuals fitting this profile all hung out together, where would you find them? This is where you place your new cards and maybe a brochure. If these people all needed services, how would they know they had a need? What kinds of symptoms would they seek services for? What kinds of benefits would appeal to them? If they were to look for help how would they know about you? Is there a local referral network such as your professional association? Are there business clubs you can join? What qualifies you to provide these services? How can you prove your expertise? If they heard about another person who had the same skills as you, why would they choose you? Are you convenient, cheap, expensive? Do you accept insurance?

You've looked at your professional strengths, and the attributes of your ideal client. Now analyze your marketing tools. The following list summarizes a variety of marketing vehicles:

Brochures
Bylines
Cable TV show
Calendar listings
Computer on-line networking
Contacts (lunch)
Drop-in discussion groups
Grand opening of your office
Lectures
Media releases
Networking
New services announcements
Newsletters
Other announcements
Paid advertising
Publications
Public service events
Radio
Speaking
Special events
Teaching
Videotape
Workshops

Figure 5.1

Professional Strengths

Stage 1

How Would You Describe Yourself as a Professional?

Stage 2

Describe your:

Chosen treatment methodologies.
Diagnosis you are most successful with.
Other models you work with.

Stage 3

How Would You Describe Your Own Expertise?

Stage 4

In What Other Arenas Have You Noticed Opportunities Where You Could Be of Value?

Stage 5

What New Roles Have You Begun to Develop?

Which of these marketing vehicles have you used with success? Which ones were a disappointment? If you can answer these questions, you have all the information you need to start your marketing plan: You know who you are, who constitute your market, how to reach them, how you can let them know about you, why they can trust you to provide quality services, and why they would choose you rather than another professional. Now reach out to them.

Rule out any marketing vehicles you have used that did not work for you and consider using another marketing vehicle. Ask yourself why your previous efforts did not work. Did you pursue them long enough? Usually, seven to nine contacts are necessary before most people make a buying decision. All these contacts can mean up to 24 weeks of advertising or mailings. Were you targeting the wrong audience? Did you put your marketing materials in the wrong places?

The worksheet shown in Figure 5.2 lists all of these ideas and is a general marketing analysis. Tasks are broken under each heading into smaller parts. The questions identified are listed in the order of what needs to be evaluated first, and the general ease of accomplishment. For example, it is generally easier for people to assess and buy advertising than to plan for and deliver public speaking. Customize your marketing approach by matching your current skills to the marketing activities you believe can best promote your business.

I suggest you go over the outline and create 3-by-5-inch index cards or a database. As you answer each arena, you will think of marketing ideas. Write each down on an index card. At first, they don't need to be in any kind of order. Later, you will begin to categorize them in the following ways:

- *Ideas I Can Implement Now.* These are the marketing activities you feel comfortable doing today.
- *Future Plans.* These seem like good ideas, but are not feasible right now. Go over these cards monthly. You will find the things you felt uncomfortable about yesterday don't seem so difficult today. Ideally, you will keep putting more and more cards into the "Ideas I Can Implement Now" file.

When you have a pile of cards for ideas you can use now, begin to cost them out. What will each activity cost you in time, money, or other resources? Identify how much you would enjoy the activity. After prioritizing the activities by enjoyment and cost, it's up to you to decide what is most important. I prefer to do something that may cost me more time but that I enjoy, than to choose something that is cheap in time and money, but isn't much fun.

Sometimes it is helpful to spread out your cards for usable ideas where you can see them all at once. Pick them up in the order you want to work on them. You have the beginnings of your marketing plan.

All you need to do now is schedule when you will do what. You can be working on more than one activity at a time. You can buy one of those big yearly planning calendars and put it up on the wall or buy a good project planning software package. What you want to do is create tasks for yourself to develop each marketing goal. Some will happen soon, and others will require more time for development. If you work on only the short-term goals now, you won't have anything with more depth happening in the future. Nevertheless, I highly recommend short-term goals for everyone. You need the immediate feedback

Figure 5.2

Marketing Assessment Worksheet

Gathering Information

Primary Customer Profile

Create a market analysis for each target population you will be reaching out to. Make a separate list for each market giving the following demographics:

- Age.
- Income.
- Sex.
- Marital status.
- Size of household.
- Education.
- Geographic location.
- Special issues.
- Reading or information-gathering habits.
- Profession(s).
- Leisure activities.
- Presenting problem.

Description of Current Market for Your Products or Services

Market Evolution

How has the market changed and where do you believe it is going?

(Continued)

Figure 5.2 *(Continued)*

Competition

What services do competing services offer and what are their fees?

Industry Trends

Looking at the field from a larger framework, what is changing?

Positioning

What is your place in the marketplace you have described?

Unique Selling Principle (USP)

What makes your product(s) or service(s) different from others offering similar product(s) or service(s)?

Packaging

Is all your printed material congruent? Do you have a graphic identity and consistent delivery of printed materials? Identify the items you have in place and decide which ones are consistent with your graphic identity.

Business Stationery

- Business card.
- Letterheads.
- Envelopes:
    - Return.
    - General business.

(Continued)

Figure 5.2 *(Continued)*

- Labels.
- Billing statements.
- FAX cover sheet.
- Brochures:

  General.
  Personal qualifications to practice profession.
  Informational.
  Event specific.
- Pamphlets.
- Books.
- Flyers and posters.
- Signs:

  Do your internal and external signs have a graphic identity?
  Are they consistent?
- Web page.

Advertising

Does your advertising maintain a graphic identity?

Products

Do your products carry your graphic identity theme throughout?

Paid Advertising

- Newsletters.
- Periodical publications.
- Magazines.
- Radio.
- Television.

(Continued)

Figure 5.2 *(Continued)*

Networking

Develop scripts so your verbal message is consistent. Make them for the audiences you believe you will be addressing:

- Family and friends.
- Business acquaintances.
- Colleagues.
- Other professionals.
- Specific target audiences.

Resource Directory

Develop a personal resource directory of people you would use as referrals.

Teaching

Internet

Media Releases

Calendar Listings

- Newspapers.
- Newsletters.
- Magazines.
- Weekly throwaways.

(Continued)

Figure 5.2 *(Continued)*

Events

- Personal events that relate to service(s).
- New services.
- Drop-in discussion groups.
- Public forums.
- Workshops and seminars.
- Lectures.
- Bylines.
- Radio spots.
- Videotape.

Television

- Broadcast.
- Cable.

Publications

- Announcements.
  - Opening office.
    - Who you are.
    - What you offer.
    - Date of open house.
  - New services.
- Documentation for new services:
  - Cover letter.
  - Flyer.
  - Fact sheet or brochure.
  - Media releases.

(Continued)

Figure 5.2 *(Continued)*

- Brochures:
  General professional (e.g., APA, NASW, AMHCA, AAMFT) information.
  Personal qualifications for practicing profession.
- Newsletters:
  Behavioral healthcare.
  Private sector.
  Specialty.
- Return postcards for:
  Informational brochures.
  Prevention information.
  Self-assessments.
- Bylines.
- Journal articles.
- Books.

Training

- Pilot programs.

Products

- Audio- and videotapes.
- Books.
- CD-ROM.

On-Line Services

- Informational.
- Educational.
- Consultive.

(Continued)

Figure 5.2 *(Continued)*

Public Speaking Press Kit

Include samples of any or all of the preceding items in a folder with your personal and business name on it. Give it to people to help them understand you and your work in a comprehensive manner.

Goals

Based on the information you have gathered, what are your:

- Long-term goals?
- Short-term goals?

Plan

Arrange your long-term and short-term goals in order of importance. Order them separately. You may find that your long-term goals can be broken into smaller goals. You may also find short-term goals that have no relation to your long-term goals. To begin, simply create separate lists. You can integrate them as a second phase. Once you have made a prioritized list of your goals, create a time line for taking action.

Budget

Attach budgets to your action items. Create a time and a money budget. Some activities will demand more time and others more money. There will probably be a trade-off between things you can't afford and things that will require more of your time. If you have the money, you can cut short your time expenses. After you create your budget, look again at your plan to see whether you need to readjust the time line.

in the beginning to convince yourself marketing is worthwhile.

CHECKING OUT HOW YOU ARE DOING

I'm a firm believer in reality checks. At the end of the work week, I take time to review what I have done and what I can learn from it. At the end of each week, ask yourself:

- How many new contacts did I make this week?
- Of those contacts, which ones do I feel good about?
- Which ones will develop into a potential new customer?
- In what ways do those potential customers stand out?
- What do those new customers have in common?
- What did I learn from the contacts that did not result in further connection: What got in the way of our potential relationship? What could I do differently with this type of individual next time?

Review your marketing plan regularly and revise it as needed.

6

MAKING THE MOST OF YOUR MARKETING TOOLS

Are You Ready for Success?

Before you bring people flocking to your doors with your marketing efforts, consider the following:

- Is your office conveniently located for your target clients?
- Can you provide adequate parking?
- Do you need a waiting room?
- Will you be able to return calls promptly?
- Do you want to do telephone consultations if clients can't come to your office and will you have time for such consultations?
- Are your office or workshop hours convenient for customers and clients?
- Do you have client satisfaction or evaluation forms ready?
- Are you ready to track referral sources as well as the other ways clients hear about your services or products?
- For those who respond to your marketing piece, what next service or product can you develop for them?

Success is great, but if you aren't prepared for the best you will be wasting time and sending a marketing message of less than optimal services. Make certain you are ready for success.

Before You Start

Before you start your marketing campaign, you need to prepare a business plan and develop a marketing plan (see Chapters 2–5). Now you are ready to act on your marketing efforts using the three key steps:

1. *Establish Goals:*

   How many new clients do you want?

   How many students do you want in your training course or adult education class?

How many booklets do you want to sell?

This is the single most important part of marketing. Set some goals now! Remember, they must be SMART (Specific, Measurable, Accessible, Realistic, Timely).

2. *Design Your Message:*

   What benefits will your new clients or customers receive from your products or services? List at least three and try them out on others to see if they are really benefits, or just what you think is important.

   What makes your services unique or different from your competition? Don't disparage other professionals, only describe why your services may be a better match for your potential customers.

3. *Reach the Right Audience:*

   Who is your ideal client or customer?

   Where are such persons likely to hear about you?

   What publications do they read?

   Where can you network with them?

Beware of self-indulgent creativity in your marketing efforts. Marketing is a dialectic. You must present every new idea to an objective critic and listen to the response. You may have a beautifully executed design for your logo, but if your audience does not know what you are trying to communicate, it is of little value. Carry this warning with you in every marketing effort you make.

START HERE

Steps 1 and 2 were covered in previous chapters. You also envisioned your ideal client. Now your task is to reach that client. Referrals, referrals, referrals: How do you get them? All professionals want to know about the resources in their region. They need to know of other professionals they can refer to when a client's problem is outside their area of expertise. A *resource directory* helps expand your knowledge of resources and offers a way for others to get to know you. Before you start on your directory, however, define your specialties and have a business card prepared.

THE RESOURCE DIRECTORY

The resource directory serves a twofold purpose. First it is your insurance that you know about all the resources in your area, or outside if needed, to provide referrals for your clients' needs. Second, it is your way of letting others know who you are and where your office is located. As you create the directory, you will meet and begin to dialogue with professionals working in the same arenas, and in collateral businesses that offer supportive or secondary need services or products. For example, if your specialty is eating disorders, you will want to have a list of nutritionists and maybe stores where women who wear very large sizes can shop for attractive clothing. There may be a support group at a local agency or an eating disorder self-help group in your area. I'm sure you can think of more. This will be a source of referrals and increasing knowledge about your area of expertise.

Getting Started

Begin by setting up a binder, card file, or database where you can organize your information and handle referrals or return calls with a knowledgable response. When you set up your files, you may want to organize them strictly alphabetically or by area of expertise. If you create a database, this means identifying fields; if you use a binder or card file, you will have dividers. Figure 6.1 contains a starter list of specialty areas.

Next, put together a Directory Worksheet like the one in Figure 6.2 to send to others or to organize your information on.

This worksheet is designed to be sent to a resource to fill out and return. Personalize yours so you gather all the information you believe is important in your area of specialization.

Choosing Your Vehicle

Once you've set your goals, designed your message, and gathered your resource directory, you need to figure out the best vehicles for marketing or promoting your services. Marketing vehicles

Figure 6.1

Specialty Areas

Abortion
Abuse
Abuse—child
Abuse—elder
Abuse—spousal
Adolescent(s)
Adoption
Adult daycare
Adult services
Advocacy
Aftercare
AIDS
Alcohol treatment
Ambulances
Animal shelters
Animal welfare
Arbitration
Art therapy
Autism
Bereavement
Bilingual issues
Biofeedback
Birth defects
Blind services
Child care
Child counseling
Compulsions
Counseling
Crisis
Deaf services
Dental
Depression

(Continued)

Figure 6.1 *(Continued)*

Detox
Divorce
Domestic violence
Drop-in treatment
Employee assistance program
Eating disorders
Families
Financial assistance
Food distribution
Foster care
Gay(s)
Group
Disabled populations
Health club
Hearing impaired
Help lines
Homeless shelter
Hospice
Housing
Hypnosis
Incest
Information and referral
Interpreters
Learning disabilities
Lesbian(s)
Men's organization
Mortuary
Music therapy
Nonprofit
Nutritionist
Outpatient
Outplacement
Parents' services
Phobias
Private industry
Probation
Psychodiagnostics
Rape counseling
Respite
Rest homes
School
Self-help
Senior services
Sex counseling
Single parents
Singles
Sliding scale
Smoking cessation
Stress management
Suicide
Support groups
Victims
Women's organization
Women's services
Youth services

Figure 6.2

Resource Directory Worksheet

Date: ___________ New ______ Revision ______

Specialty Category of Resource: ______________________________

Contact name: ______________________________

Business name: ______________________________

Address: ______________________________

City, State, Zip: ______________________________

Telephone(s): ______________________________

Hours of service: ______________________________

Population(s) served: Include languages spoken and special needs provided for. Are you wheelchair accessible? ______________________________

Services/Products: Include specialties or special techniques you use. ______________________________

____

Credentials of professional providers: Include licensure, board certification, or other credentialing or licensing of your profession: ______________________________

Malpractice insurance: ______________________________

Fees: Indicate if you use a sliding fee scale or other forms of payment options (e.g., credit cards, payment plans): ______________________________

Insurances accepted: ______________________________

Notes: ______________________________

____

Figure 6.3

Professional Letters

To a New Professional in the Area

Dear Dr. Smith,

It is good to see a new cardiologist in our area. I have at least three clients a month who need to have a physical examination. Many are overweight, and often they are smokers. Please send me some of your business cards that I can give to these clients.

I have included information about my practice. I also have information brochures about many topics in mental health. If I can be of any help to you, please give me a call. Welcome to Boston.

To a Referring Colleague

Dear Dr. Jones,

I received a call the other day from an individual needing counseling. He told me it was upon your recommendation. Thank you for the referral. Referrals from colleagues are very rewarding.

If you have any materials about your practice, brochures, flyers, please send them to me. Thanks again.

(which will be discussed in detail in this chapter) include personal letters, direct mail brochures and packages, and business cards. Chapter 7 will cover less direct ways of getting the word out such as authoring, electronic media, public speaking, promotional events, and other media.

Printed Material

Once you have a resource list, you need to maintain contact with the people in your file or database. Printed material is a good way of staying in touch. You can use many kinds of printed material as a marketing tool. Some you may not have thought were marketing pieces but simply office supplies. Printed material is just what it sounds like, anything printed: mailings, your business cards, office stationery, and any other printed matter that relates to your business. Everything that can be written can be used as some kind of marketing piece. Here are some ideas:

- Send out a personal letter introducing yourself and your practice to professionals in your region or area of specialty.
- Send thank-you notes or letters to referral sources.
- Send progress reports to your referral sources (with written releases).
- Send discharge notes to referral sources. These are usually not required or requested. It is a way to keep your name in their mind so that, when they have someone to refer, they think of you.
- Send reprints of articles to new professionals in your region and to your current referral sources. When I read something and it reminds me of a business contact, I cut it out and drop it in the mail to that person. It doesn't cost me much time or money, but it is a way of saying *you are important to me.*
- Send consumer survey outcomes to referral sources who are interested in your specialty.

These are just a few ideas. The marketing tools in Figure 6.3 are great ways of keeping your professional identity in the current mind-set of colleagues and referral sources.

Your letters don't need to be long. The goal is to make as many connections with potential referral sources as possible.

Both personal letters and formal brochures have pros and cons (Figure 6.4).

DIRECT MAIL OUTREACH

Direct mail has been the most approachable project for those who are new to marketing. It doesn't require direct marketing or sales experience. You can almost pretend you aren't really marketing. You should, however, come out of the closet at least long enough to do market research on your direct mail piece before sending off an expensive mailing.

Direct mail means exactly what it sounds like: You are mailing your message, advertising, or request directly to each targeted individual. Direct-mail packages include combinations of letters, brochures, cards, literature, flyers, response forms, samples, and offerings. Samples of some of these materials are included in this chapter. Documents are also available on disc for your computer and can be used with your letterhead or preprinted desktop masters. Some sources are:

Figure 6.4

Printed Material

Advantages	Disadvantages
Personal letters	
Personal letters are inexpensive.	One letter is usually not enough. It must be followed up with additional material or a personal contact.
You can say specific things about yourself and command the attention of the reader.	You must write clearly and have correct spelling and grammar.
Brochures	
Referral sources may ask for one. If you have one prepared, you are ahead of others.	Your costly brochure may get thrown in the round file.
A brochure informs people in more depth about who you are and what you do.	If you are good at self-marketing and individual contacts, you may not need a brochure.

- PaperDirect: 1-800-PAPERS.
- Queblo: 1-800-523-9080.
- Beaver Prints: 1-800-BEAVER (232-8374).
- Premier Papers: 1-800-843-0414.
- Impact: 1-800-433-2278.

Direct mail, with the development of a referral base, serves multiple purposes:

- To introduce yourself and establish initial contact.
- To establish yourself as an expert in some specialty.
- To establish a reputation.
- To follow up and to follow through after initial contacts.
- To lay the groundwork for other contacts.

Direct-mail materials are combined in various ways to fulfill these purposes.

DIRECT-MAIL VEHICLES

Brochures

You get brochures everywhere these days. You too can have one. Of the several kinds of brochures around, a few styles are particularly appropriate for professionals:

- General or personal brochure.
- Informational brochure.
- Specialty brochure.
- Special event brochure.

The Design

The *personal business brochure* is usually 8½ by 11 inches and is folded twice equidistantly along the long side. This results in six panels and a size convenient for a business envelope and one first-class postage stamp. If it were entirely filled with text (which it shouldn't be), the brochure could contain about 1,800 words or nine double-spaced typewritten pages. The length of the message on a brochure of this type is about equal to a person's attention span. If you can't state your message in these six panels, you need to rethink what it is you are marketing.

The best way to think through your message is to take a blank sheet of paper, fold it into the six panels, and put a different message on each panel. For example:

- *Cover Panel.* A graphic and your name and address and telephone number. Include some message that prompts the reader to open it up.
- *Left Inside Panel.* A recitation of 12 one-liner needs and benefits related to what you are selling.
- *Center Inside Panel.* Your experience and training.
- *Right Inside Panel.* Symptoms for which people might seek your help and summary of the information from the other panels.
- *Left Outside Panel.* An immodest description of your professional accomplishments and/or affiliations or your philosophical or theoretical approach to your work. You can have a photo of yourself accompanied by approximately 200 words of prose to establish who you are and what you are about.
- *Left Inside or Back Mailer Panel.* The address panel. If this is a mailer you put your return address in the upper left-hand corner. If you are using a bulk mail permit it goes in the top right-hand corner. You can put a tickler statement on the front to get people to open it. If it is not a mailer, use benefit statements or testimonials since this panel is highly visible.

Figure 6.5 describes the layout of a brochure.

It is imperative that you check with your professional organization to make certain you are following their ethics and guidelines for advertising. They may have restrictions not only in content but also on distribution. Some professional associations have preprinted brochures for members, with an area where they can place their business information. It's safe to say that the use of some brochures under some circumstances is possible. This marketing piece may give you a competitive advantage over the professional down the street who doesn't have one.

If you are trying to get on approved provider lists, you can use a brochure as a supplementary

Figure 6.5

Items Included in a Brochure Layout

Left Outside Panel	Left Inside Panel or Back (Mailer) Panel	Cover
This panel is often used to highlight: Key Benefits. Endorsements. Present empathetic statements. Graphics or photos. Usually folds inward.	When a brochure is a "self-mailer," postal information goes here frequently with a teaser statement that highlights a special offer or benefit. On non-self-mailers, organizational descriptions, logo, address, and phone information are often placed here.	Usually, a brief benefit statement or question, and/or graphic or photo goes here—perhaps your name and logo. Allow plenty of white space. Remember, all you're trying to do is get the recipient to open the brochure.

Left Inside Panel	Center Inside Panel	Right Inside (Sell) Panel
This panel should pick up on the cover theme. When presenting the who's, what's, and why's of your service or product, use benefits language!	**Benefits.** What is benefits language? Rather than describing yourself or your service, tell potential clients what they will receive or be able to do by using your services or product(s). Don't oversell!	**Summarize.** Tell them clearly how, when, and where to respond. Keep it simple. Offer encouragement. Reach out. Always put yourself in your potential client's shoes.

device to secure that position. A brochure is more interesting to look at than a resume; it even allows you to brag selectively about yourself in the third person. Brochure costs can range from inexpensive products of your own computer, to costly designs by a graphic artist. In the beginning, you can use an economical but attractive brochure made through desktop publishing. You can order quality preprinted paper and the computer templates for the layout from the companies listed earlier in this chapter.

After you have a sense of what you want, I highly recommend you go to a good graphic artist in your area and order a professionally designed brochure. If there is no one in your area, I recommend AdVentures, the graphic designers for the Family Therapy Networker (tel. 1-800-262-2221).

Imagination and talent are used in the design of the brochure. This includes the selection of the words, drawings, text, quotes, photos, maps, or whatever communicates your message. Collect and look at the brochures that attract your attention. Call the person who produced the brochure and ask who put it together.

General or Personal Business Brochure

A business card leaves a small impression. The personal business brochure (see Figure 6.6) describes, in more detail, your practice and the general services of your business. Begin with who you are and include the love and joy you feel about your work. Put into words the way you have designed your business and services to serve your clients' needs. Effective marketing expresses the commitment, identity, uniqueness, and value you bring to your business. The primary goal is to communicate a business identity consistent with your personal values and approaches in a way that produces growth for you, your clients, and your practice. Use the feedback you receive about your brochure from clients and colleagues, to find what they value about your work. Continue to refine the brochure as you and your work grow and change.

The Informational Brochure

These brochures feature a small piece of psychoeducation. They usually identify a specific specialty area and offer general information and potential resources for services or products. The informational brochure can be mailed to resources who can use them themselves, or you can hand them out to those in need. You can leave them in your waiting room and ask others to do the same. Figure 6.7 shows an example of an informational brochure. Use the following format:

1. *Opening.* A general introduction to the topic.
2. *Definition of Problem.* How would the public know whether this problem existed? Remember to use lay terms, not the ones you read in your professional journals. Your local public library will probably have a self-help book in this area. Reading it will give you a sense of how to explain the topic to the public.
3. *How the Problem Develops.* Use lay language again. Include vignettes relating the problem to behavior and experiences other people have had. Of course you won't use any experiences of your clients. You never know who will read it, especially in a limited distribution area such as a small town.

Figure 6.6

Personal Added-Business Brochure

Linda S. Lawless, M.A., MFCC
CA State License No. MF 21588

I strive to improve the overall quality of living and dedicate myself to expertise in my field. I commit to the education required to stay on the leading edge of the exploration and discovery of human potential.

If I can be of help to you or someone you care about, call today for immediate assistance, information or an appointment.

Personally Speaking

Your decision to seek counseling heralds a turning point in your life. In our rapidly changing world, people often seek professional guidance to remain on an even keel.

BULK RATE
US POSTAGE
PAID
BENICIA, CA
PERMIT NO. 65

Linda S. Lawless, M.A., MFCC
845 First Street
P.O. Box 1884
Benicia, CA 94510
707/747-9550

& Personally Speaking ...

Linda S. Lawless, M.A., MFCC
845 First Street
Benicia, CA 94510

by appointment
707/747-9550

As your world becomes busier and more fast-paced, emotional strain can lead to confusion and stress. Occasionally you may find a need for guidance and support. Counseling can help ease your journey down a bumpy road.

When to seek counseling

When you have used all your resources and find that any of the following affect your personal or professional life in a destructive way, counseling can help you learn more effective ways to handle:

- **Addictive behaviors** - overuse of food, alcohol, drugs, sex, work; co-dependence or "loving too much."
- **Emotional problems** - grief, depression, excessive anger or jealousy, anxiety, phobias, or panic attacks.
- **Relationship problems** - difficulties in getting along with co-workers; emotional, sexual or communication problems; difficulty initiating and/or maintaining relationships; divorce.
- **Stress/Individual** - related to major life transitions, job "burn-out," or general life overload.
- **Stress/Organizational** - individuals working at cross purposes to the goals of the group.
- **Low self-esteem** - feelings of insecurity, shyness, worthlessness; unhappiness with physical presence (overweight).
- **Family issues** - parenting difficulties, step-family blending, difficult children, aging parents, adult child of a dysfunctional family.
- **Life's challenges** - personal and spiritual growth, career development, midlife crisis, women's issues.

Remember, substance abuse, family issues, emotional disorders and other personal problems can have a serious negative effect on a person's life. Treatment, rather than discipline, is a more comprehensive, longer lasting, cost effective approach.

Counseling Services

All appointments are confidential.

Individual counseling helps you gain insight into the cause of your problems and seek positive alternatives.

Couples counseling provides an arena where two people can learn to communicate individual needs and negotiate a healthy partnership.

Premarital counseling can help pave the way to a partnership that grows and lasts.

Marriage counseling can create understanding and communication in your marriage and encourage you to overcome marital difficulties.

Family counseling helps family members gain an understanding of disruptive problems. Improved communication skills provide new ways to reach solutions that lead to greater family harmony.

Groups

Treatment groups led by a licensed therapist provide you with an opportunity to openly discuss your problems in a supportive environment. The group setting enables you to learn from the experiences of others.

Self-help groups provide the ongoing support of a group of people with similar issues. If one is not available in your area of interest, I will help you set one up.

Prevention

Peak performance in any situation requires both physical and mental fitness. Ongoing education and daily practice/s ensure a higher quality of life.

Training

- Assertiveness
- Career Development
- Communication Skills
- Fair Fighting
- Mental Fitness
- Single Parenting
- Self Management & Personal Organization
- Stress Management

Self Help Library & Resource Center

I have made a commitment to filling community mental health needs by providing in-house treatment and training programs, a self-help resource center, and a referral network to other community resources.

I maintain a safe, confidential place for individuals in crisis or life transitions to talk, sort out issues, and create new solutions to old problems.

Convenient

Most Insurances Accepted
Call 707/747-9550
Help can be a phonecall away

Figure 6.7

Informational Brochure

LINDA L. LAWLESS, LMFT LMHC

I strive to improve the overall quality of living and dedicate myself to expertise in my field. I commit to the education required to stay on the leading edge of the exploration and discovery of human potential.

If I can be of help to you or someone you care about, call today for immediate assistance, information or an appointment.

Personally Speaking

Your decision to seek counseling heralds a turning point in your life. In our rapidly changing world, people often seek professional guidance to remain on an even keel.

BULK RATE
U.S. POSTAGE
PAID
BENICIA, CA
PERMIT NO. 65

Linda L. Lawless LMFT LMHC
25 Huntington Avenue Suite 520
Boston MA 02116

617.662.6026

& Personally Speaking ...

Eating Disorders

LINDA L. LAWLESS, LMFT LMHC
25 Huntington Avenue Suite 520
Boston MA 02116

by appointment
617.662.6026

INFORMATIONAL SERIES

BINGE EATING DISORDER (BED)

BINGE EATING DISORDER(BED)

Characterized by recurrent episodes of greatly excessive eating accompanied by feelings of being uncomfortably full, loss of control, self-depreciation, which occurs at least two times a week for six months or more. Different from Bulimia, there is no purging. Other characteristics can be extreme distress afterward; eating more rapidly than usual; eating despite not being hungry; eating large amounts throughout the day without regard to mealtimes; eating alone out of embarrassment; and experiencing post-binge feelings of self-disgust.

Binge eating was described in the medical literature over 30 years ago but has not been included in the traditional diagnostic indices as separate from Bulimia or Anorexia. Dr. Robert Spitzer of Columbia University's New York State Psychiatric Institute in NY City conducted a nationwide survey of 4,000 men and women and found that two percent of the general population and four percent of college students fit the clinical description of BED.

Binge eaters tend to develop weight problems at a younger age than nonbingers, and experience more weight cycling over the course of their lives. Women are more likely to exhibit BED behaviors. In fact, three women for every two men are diagnosed with this disorder. It has been noted that women are under more pressure to be thin and tend to assign more meanings to food than men do. Women often turn to food for solace while men may turn to other things, like work, drugs or alcohol.

The precise cause of BED is still unclear. Experts agree that emotional and biological factors are probably to blame. People with BED have a higher incidence of clinical depression, researchers are not sure if they eat because they are depressed or are depressed because of their eating. They also tend to have lower self-esteem than nonbingers.

TREATMENT

Some studies suggest that antidepressant drug therapy can reduce the frequency of bingeing episodes. Others argue that BED is primarily a genetic issue. It is also clear that other issues such as social and psychological factors also play a role in the development of this disorder. Rather than focusing on how to loose weight, clinicians are beginning to focus on ways to deal with the bingeing rather than simply cutting calories. Strict diets fail because they leave people feeling deprived and eventually trigger a binge.

The NIH, National Institute of Health in Bethesda has developed a six step BED treatment program:

First, subjects are told to stop stringently regulating their food intake. Then, researchers help them establish normal balanced eating habits since people with BED typically skip breakfast, have a very light lunch, then start bingeing in the late afternoon or evening. Planning and eating a sensible breakfast, lunch and dinner can help head off the hunger that leads to bingeing.
Third, bingers reexamine their life priorities.
Fourth, they are helped to work on building relationships instead of turning to food for support Bingers often use food as a way of dealing with other things they're distressed over.
Fifth, physical activity is emphasized

Finally, the acceptance of weight and self and getting rid of negative mental scripts is supported.

PREVENTION

Almost everybody has had an experience of "binge eating." If bingeing is becoming more frequent here are some ideas that are wise for just about everybody.

1 — Don't skip meals. Learn to hear and honor your bodies "hunger signals." Eat when you are hungry and stop when you are full.

2 — Spread the intake of heavily laden caloric foods. No foods are "bad" but some are higher in fats and sugar than others. Think about portion sizes. For example a smaller piece of chocolate cake might be filling than the same size piece of angel food cake. Also by thinking about and choosing portion sizes we gain more of a sense of control over our eating habits.

3 — Learn which emotions and situations trigger a binge and develop an alternative coping or self soothing strategy. For example, if you tend to binge when you are bored, start going for a walk instead of eating. If you binge with you are having difficulty in your relationship, find a friend or other resource where you can honestly talk about your feelings.

4 — Try to plan your meals based on your personal needs and eat with others you enjoy. When you learn to listen to your body and it's biological and emotional needs, you will begin to get a sense of what diet choices you need to make. There are also seasonal factors to include. Learn about nutrition. There are many approaches to nutrition. Take yourself to the library and begin to get a sense of the many different way's wo/man has explored the use of food not only as a nutritional source but also a healing resource.

5 — Exercise regularly. A simple 15 minute walk three times a week can help you feel better and more in control. You will fine that when you feel good about yourself and your ability to make choices in your life you are less likely to binge.

4. *Checklist for Symptoms.* This list needs to be short and concise. You have already talked about the problem definition and how it develops. Here is where you crystallize the symptoms.
5. *Strategies for Dealing with the Problem.* Offer alternative solutions and relate them to the scenarios you created earlier.
6. *References for Additional Reading and Information.* Your reference librarian can be helpful here. You want to offer books, tapes, and magazine articles as well as people and places.
7. *Summary.* This summarizes all of the preceding information and includes something personal about you. You want to relate all this information to your professional practice and its services and products.
8. *Standard Design—Different Colors.* If you have more than one specialty, you may want to create several informational brochures, but keep a standard graphic identity in all of them. I know a professional who uses such brochures extensively and has a rainbow of colors for varying themes. It is easy to identify the source of these brochures because each one has a similar cover; only the theme differs. She keeps them in her waiting room and offers them to others in bulk, for printing costs only.
9. *Logo on Back Panel Where Readers Were Referred to Other Resources.* When you list resources, be sure to include yourself. Include all the information the reader will need to connect with you. Include at least your name, address, and telephone number (also fax and e-mail address if you have them). Include hours of operation and credit card and insurance you accept as well.
10. *Subjects.* Here are some subjects for informational brochures you might want to explore:
    - Time and activities management.
    - Stress management.
    - Understanding depression.
    - Permanent weight control.
    - Assertive communication.
    - Suicide prevention in teens.
    - Helping a troubled relationship.
    - Gambling.
    - Burnout.
    - Substance abuse.
    - Parenting problems.
    - The importance of self-esteem.
    - Conflict resolution.
    - Facing a crisis.

Specialty Brochure

This brochure identifies a particular specialty you are declaring. I suggest you first develop your general business brochure and then create specialty brochures for more strategic marketing. Some professionals want to be identified only with one specialty although I think this is a long-term risk. That specialty area may lose its market value or you may want to change after several years in one area. Having a general position that you can leverage off is a more long-term solution.

People sometimes put inserts in their general brochure but I don't think this is effective unless it is well tied into the brochure. Be sure you maintain some kind of graphic identity throughout all your marketing pieces. Your specialty brochure can follow the same general format of your general brochure but will include specialty-specific information (see Figure 6.8 for an example of a specialty brochure). This brochure is different from the information brochure because it includes information about a specific problem.

Special Event Brochure

Special event brochures are tied to specific workshops, books, and special events (see Figure 6.9 for a sample special event promotional piece). Make sure you carry your graphic theme throughout all your brochures unless the special event is in collaboration with another group. Be sure to include a mail-back piece so people can:

- Register.
- Ask to be put or maintained on your mailing list for future mailings.

Special Design Brochures

There is no end to the creativity of graphic designers and the ingenuity of printers. There are brochures that have a tear-off mailer, a Rolodex card that can be torn out, or a postcard that can be torn out. There are also *step-up* brochures that include inserts printed in graduated heights so you can see the top portion of several cards, each with different information on it. The only limit is your imagination.

How to Think through Your Brochure

Before you prepare your own brochures, you need to answer two questions:

1. Whom are you talking to in your brochure?
2. What are you trying to sell?

Chapters 3 through 5 in this book can help you pinpoint your answers to these critical questions. Next you should start collecting samples of brochures. Write or call people in the same business to get their brochures. Go to brochure libraries, which can be found at printers, consultants, associations, and professional organizations, and consult the examples in this book. Now start writing. Do a mock layout (even if it's just on copy paper). Show your brochure to others for objective suggestions (try a nine-year-old to see if he or she gets the point, or find a newspaper reporter, who will cut out the redundancies). Don't agonize over all the decisions, just create a rough draft. Business associates or other acquaintances can help you refine it.

Letters

Brochures are a lot more effective if they are accompanied by a cover letter. You can write a short letter in any of the following situations and include one of your brochures with it:

- To say you have a mutual connection and to introduce yourself.
- To remind someone of a previous contact and that you would like to get together again.
- To follow up on a previous contact.
- To say you practice in the same area and want to introduce yourself and your work.
- To offer referrals in general or a referral specifically.
- To say you practice in a related specialty and want to introduce yourself and your work.

Figure 6.8

Speciality Brochure

LINDA L. LAWLESS, LMFT LMHC

I strive to improve the overall quality of living and dedicate myself to expertise in my field. I commit to the education required to stay on the leading edge of the exploration and discovery of human potential.

If I can be of help to you or someone you care about, call today for immediate assistance, information or an appointment.

Personally Speaking

Your decision to seek counseling heralds a turning point in your life. In our rapidly changing world, people often seek professional guidance to remain on an even keel.

BULK RATE
U.S. POSTAGE
PAID
BENICIA, CA
PERMIT NO. 65

Linda L. Lawless, LMFT LMHC
25 Huntington Avenue, Suite 520
Boston MA 02116

& Personally Speaking ...

LINDA L. LAWLESS, LMFT LMHC
25 Huntington Avenue, Suite 520
Boston MA 02116

by appointment
617.662.6026

Specialty

Eating Disorders

I approach eating disorders in women from a foundation of women's distinctive psycho-social developmental process. I believe that women with eating disorders heal and grow most effectively in a safely constructed therapeutic setting that emphasizes the development of trust in the counselor and the counseling process. I believe effective treatment, that creates lasting change, honors the individual's life experiences and collaborates with and draws on the client's cognitive and emotional wisdom to choose what is "right" for them in their "next step" in the healing process.

Being a systems-oriented therapist I believe I must also pay attention to the differing systems the client involves themselves with, i.e., families, ethnic, racial and socio-economic groups and religious groups and belief systems.

Other aspects of women's lives such as age, presence or absence of children, professional identity and sexual orientation (heterosexual, homosexual or bisexual) also needs to be explored and acknowledged in their impact on the development of the particular eating disorder.

I do not apply a generic treatment methodology to my clients. I consider the background and circumstance of each eating disordered women to provide her with the safety, guidance and support she needs to recover. I also know I must continually explore and be aware of my own position in relation to my clients, i.e., countertransference, racial, cultural, sexual or other personal or systemic issues that impact treatment.

Finally, my work is wholistic in nature. I pay attention to verbal, nonverbal and behavioral communications. I also look at the physical, mental, emotional, relational, professional and spiritual aspects of each client's life.

For more information regarding Eating Disorders please call my office for a Reading List @ 617.662.6026

When to seek counseling

When you have used all your resources and find that any of the following affect your personal or professional life in a destructive way, counseling can help you learn more effective ways to handle:

- **Addictive behaviors** - overuse of food, purging, excessive exersize.
- **Emotional problems** - depression, unexpressed anger or jealousy, anxiety, phobias, or panic attacks.
- **Relationship problems** - difficulties in getting along with family members; emotional, sexual or communication problems; difficulty initiating and/or maintaining relationships.
- **Stress/Individual** - related to meals or pressure from others.
- **Low self-esteem** - feelings of insecurity, shyness, worthlessness; unhappiness with physical presence in spite of weight.
- **Family issues** - difficulty dealing with family problems.
- **Life's challenges** - personal and spiritual growth.

Remember, food issues, family difficulties, emotional disorders and other personal problems can have a serious negative effect on a person's life. Treatment, rather than discipline, is a more comprehensive, longer lasting, cost effective approach.

Counseling Services

All appointments are confidential.

Individual counseling helps you gain insight into the cause of your problems and seek positive alternatives.

Couples counseling provides an arena where two people can learn to communicate individual needs and negotiate a healthy partnership.

Family counseling helps family members gain an understanding of disruptive problems. Improved communication skills provide new ways to reach solutions that lead to greater family harmony.

Groups

Treatment groups led by a licensed therapist provide you with an opportunity to openly discuss your problems in a supportive environment. The group setting enables you to learn from the experiences of others.

Self-help groups provide the ongoing support of a group of people with similar issues. If one is not available in your area of interest, I will help you set one up.

Convenient

Most Insurances Accepted
Call 617.662.6026
Help can be a phone call away

Figure 6.9

Special Event Brochure

Beyond Networking

Relationship Management

Contacts contribute to your success. Practicing **relationship management** takes you from a scattershot, time consuming approach, to cultivating rewarding business relationships.

Target your contacts

If everybody's your client, then nobody's your client!

Setting goals is essential.

If your purpose is murky or scattered, then business relationships will flounder. You must know what you want at each step of the way.

Positioning for referrals

When considering where to put your time and energy, ask yourself, "Who has given me the most amount of business or resources with the least amount of time and heartache? **Who are my best working relationships with?"** Now, connect with 4 or 5 people you respect in other non-competing professions who focus on the same customer base you do. When you network, describe what you do or sell in a way that highlights the benefits of your service or product. Listen to others and ask yourself how you might support one another. As you meet others who meet the criteria above, build your new business relationships in an honorable manner.

Focus on giving

If you give, you get, but not always where you gave. When you discover a problem, give ideas, resources and information. In return, the people you have helped, will help you.

Metro Boston Professional Counseling Network
Community Education Program
25 Huntington Avenue Suite 520
Boston MA 02116

New Vision

Business & Professional

Networks

Vision • Change • Integrity

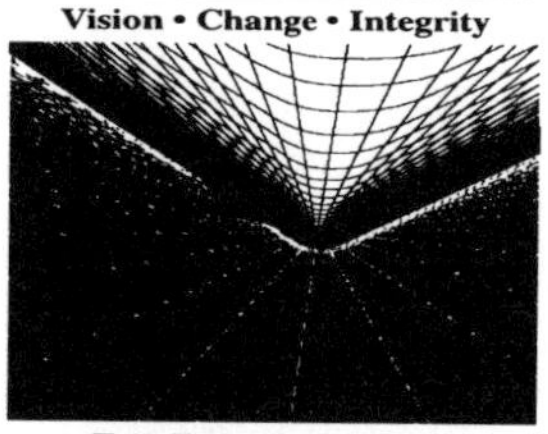

Excellence in Business

Sponsored by:
Metro-Boston Professional Counseling
Community Education Program Inc.

617/662-6026

The organization or individual that does not plan and manage the future may not have one!

Registration & Raffle Offering

Name ____________________

Business ____________________

Address ____________________

____

Telephone ____________________

FAX ____________________

E Mail ____________________

Portable Telephone ____________________

______ Yes - Please register me for June 17 Enclosed is $20.

______ Yes - I want to offer something in the Raffle. Information is attached.

______ Yes - Please keep me on your mailing list. I cannot attend on the Third Friday but I could attend on:

____________________.

Make Checks Payable to: Metro-Boston Professional Counseling

Return to: 25 HuntingtonAve., Suite 520 Boston MA 02116.

New Vision

Business & Professional

Networks

Vision • Innovation • Collaboration
&
Excellence in Business

The future belongs to those who believe in their dreams.
Eleanor Roosevelt

Networks are people talking and sharing ideas, information, and resources. NewVision Business Networks moves to the next level by creating links between people to foster self-help, exchange information and resources, and improve productivity and work life in a socially responsible manner. In the Networks environment, rewards come by empowering each other not by climbing over.

The New Vision Business Network is a supportive community of progressive-minded business professionals pursuing their personal definition of success, who are also committed to global transformation through business and social excellence. We look at the power of expectations, attitudes, and imagination in the creation of dynamic change, and support one another on our individual life/work paths.

Participants seek to develop personal leadership and other visionary habits like dealing effectively with burnout, overcoming obstacles in a healthy creative way, clearly communicating ideas, collaborating, and managing personal and professional lives towards optimal performance, balance, and peace of mind.

W5

Who Why What When Where

Participants Include

Professionals, Entrepreneurs, Educators, Service Providers, Inventors, Writers.........

Promote Your Business

This is a powerful opportunity to get the word out to an ideal market for your particular product or professional services. You will be able to display literature on networking tables, and make valuable connections during the networking periods. Bring 25 business cards, 24 to give away and one for the service raffle.

Morning Schedule

Continental breakfast
Gathering, networking
Orientation
Self-introductions
Speaker
Service raffle

The breakfasts feature dynamic, motivational speakers, chosen for their presentation quality and for the contribution they have made in their field. The service raffle features valuable services donated by participants which are given away with a drawing of business cards.

Networks functions are on the Third Friday morning of every month, from 8-9:30 AM at 25 Huntington Ave Boston MA in the Conference Room on the Third floor

$$$$$$$$

The investment for each event is $20 in advance (a check sent one week in advance is required), or $2 at the door. Make checks out to Metro-Boston Professional Counseling and send to:
25 HuntingtonAve., Suite 520 Boston MA02116.

Quality of life is becoming more of an issue than Quantity of life

- To thank someone for a referral, even though the person didn't come or you couldn't help. Include some recommendations or other referrals that might help.
- To thank someone for expressing interest and to provide requested information.
- To say thank you for someone's continuing support and interest. Describe new work you are doing or a new finding in the field, or introduce a new associate in your practice.
- To congratulate someone on the opening of a new practice or new office. State your pleasure in adding the person to your referral list. Ask when you can meet to discuss how you can help each other.
- To offer a report on a mutual patient.
- To describe the contents of the package, its purpose, and the benefits to the professional who examines them.

When I am putting together a new group or workshop, I always create a cover letter to go with my brochure. It makes it just a little more personal than a brochure in the mail. With *mail-merge* on computers, you can create a single letter and have all your names and addresses automatically inserted in the appropriate places. If you don't have the resources for mail-merge, your local desktop publishing business should be able to provide these services.

Business Cards

There are many different kinds of business cards to choose from (you thought it would be simple). Yes, you can go down to your local stationery store and order 500 or more cards printed on one side with black ink or you can consider any of the following options.

Standard Business Cards

This is your basic card with just a few additions. The card can include your name, degree, profession, address, and telephone number on one side and on the other side can list resources appropriate to your profession. You want to give people a reason to keep your card. I knew one woman who worked with eating disorders who listed a recipe for a great low-fat salad dressing on the back of her card. Another therapist listed hot line numbers, and a colleague listed self-help groups in her area of expertise. I have seen cards with inspirational pieces and even short pieces of poetry. If you want to include more information than can be printed legibly on a standard business card, you might consider the fold-over card.

Fold-Over Double Card

This card acts as a minibrochure, allowing you to be more specific about your range of services, or range within a type of service specialty. These are available from printers and are also in desktop paper supply catalogs.

Rolodex Style

Your business card is a Rolodex card, intended to be slipped among the other important and frequently used numbers in the professional's office.

Outsized Cards and Announcement Cards

Cards that are larger than the standard size or shaped differently, can make your message a lot more noticeable. Specialty designs (e.g., a card put together like a deck of cards to promote a gambler's addiction cessation program) can really catch the imagination.

Announcement Cards and Postcards

These cards can be used alone or as parts of packages. They can also be used to keep your name in the eye of your target population. Here are some examples of good reasons for sending announcements:

- Opening a new practice.
- Starting a new specialty or service.
- Taking on a new associate (or becoming a new associate).
- Opening a new office/branch.
- Giving a seminar.
- Publishing a book.
- Receiving a new degree or certification.
- Discontinuing a service or closing an office.
- Completing a major research or development project.
- Adding names to the list of practitioners to whom you make referrals.
- Having a professional anniversary.
- Having an open house.
- Offering a demonstration.

Announcement cards are sometimes sent prior to a larger brochure, or other marketing piece, telling potential clients or customers to look for another mailing or reserve a date on their calendar. These also can be purchased from printers or bought through desktop paper companies.

DIRECT-MAIL PACKAGES

Introduction/Initial Contact Packages

These should include a cover letter addressing the rationale for making the contact, your most general and comprehensive brochure, and your business card. If you have a specialty that would be the primary interest or even the sole interest of the practitioner to whom you are mailing, enclose your specialty brochure as well.

Groundwork Packages

Introduction packages are groundwork packages, of course, but many people feel better about making personal contact after more extensive warm-up. You may want to follow up your introductory package with several packages that progressively establish your reputation or expertise before you arrange a face-to-face appointment for discussing mutual interests. The contents of such packages would be as previously described. Just mix and match the various elements and organize the order of the mailings according to the kind of reputation or expertise you wish to establish. For example, if you are trying to become established as a child therapist, begin by sending an introductory package with letter, brochure, and cards. Follow through with a package containing parent education literature, samples for the professional's waiting room and a request form for other literature. Later you might send a copy of a newspaper article describing and praising your work with children. Send it along with information on a parent education seminar you are offering soon. Finally, you might send an announcement of complimentary training for pediatricians in some exciting new technique you have developed. The mailing would include a request form for training in their offices.

Mailing Planner

It is a good idea to keep track of your direct-mail pieces so there is continuity in what the identified market is receiving. Use the Mail Planner in Figure 6.10 for every mailing. Keep the sheets organized by target population with a sample of the piece you mailed behind the worksheet. Then, when you are ready to reach out to that marketplace, you can plan a marketing piece that develops logically. You will also be able to track your ROI (Return on Investment) for different pieces. Each piece should have some kind of code such as Department M3 in the return address. If there is a return card, you can record the response. If it is a call-back or referral, ask what department the piece came from.

Establishment of Expertise and Reputation

In these cases, you may or may not want to use a cover letter, or your letter itself may be the core of the package. The essential element of this kind of package is to demonstrate your expertise. It could be in the form of a research report, a piece of educational literature, or a copy of a news story or magazine article someone else has written describing your work. Pictures are often helpful when appropriate. Also, you could use a flyer, catalog, descriptive report, or picture of some material(s) or instrument(s) you have developed. The only other item you must include is something that enables the recipient to contact you; I recommend an appropriate business card. Make sure your name and address also are on the core element, whatever it is. To encourage response, I also recommend that you have a request form for further information, or an order form for material or equipment. It doesn't cost that much to add another item, but it can cost you in responses not to include one.

Follow-Up

When you're following up (completing the transactions begun in a single, immediately prior contact), you always include a cover letter reminding the recipient of the contact and of the agreement or obligation that you are fulfilling in this mailing. This essential part of establishing your reliability is the primary purpose of follow-up.

The second item you enclose will depend on the purpose of the follow-up. Did you agree to inform the recipient of something, send some literature along, provide a report? Just fulfill your promises.

If your prior contact(s) have not included the mailing or delivery of your business card or brochure, these should be included. If the recipient already has your card and brochure, include some other item that expands his or her knowledge of you or requires some sort of response that gives you an opportunity for further contact. You might include a piece of educational literature, an announcement of an upcoming seminar, a catalog of items you make available, and an order form, or a flyer on a new therapy group you are starting.

Follow-Through and Tracking

Follow-through is developing consistency or continuity of contact. Think of it as a constant linking of follow-ups. This means that the pieces

Figure 6.10

Mail Planner

Code
Target population
Type of marketing piece
Geographic location
Date sent
Package design

- Cover letter
- Brochures
- Cards
- Samples of information

Mailing List Used
Mailing Costs and Schedule

- Total no. of packages ______
- Total cost $______
- Mailing lot size ______
- Cost of mailing per lot $______
- Lot mailing schedule ______

______ Daily ______ Weekly ______ Monthly ______ Quarterly

Start Date ______

______ Entered on master mailing schedule (see Figure 6.11)

Responses Received

for follow-through are the same as follow-up, except that often the use of a cover letter is not necessary. For example, your mailer may announce the completion of a major continuing education training you have already described to your customer, complete with pictures. As with follow-up packages, telephone calls, and personal contacts, try to include something that will require an active response or leave the door open for the next contact. Use the worksheet in Figure 6.11 to list all your mailings that include the same marketing piece to more than one person.

MAILING LISTS AND DATABASES

If you are going to keep your outreach straight, you need to set up records of who receives what when. This can be done with index cards or on a computer. Templates for databases setup on Macintosh using FileMaker Pro are available from Lawless & Company (tel. 1-617-662-6026).

Mailing List Development

Computer-based systems save time after they are set up since they can create personalized mass-mailed letters using mail-merge. Using mail-merge, you can modify an outreach document by inserting the name, address, and any other information that promotes your services. Each contact name is identified with its source. To manage your database, I recommend setting up the following fields:

Master Heading—Target Population

Subheadings

- Type of practice.
- Geographic location.
- Patient population.
- Type of organization:
  - Individual.
  - Group.
  - Agency—
    - Private.
    - Public.

Master Heading—Resources

Subheadings

- Directories:
  - Yellow Pages.
  - Specialized Yellow Pages.
  - Professional organizations and associations.
  - State and national licenses.
- Previous contact lists.
- Government agencies.
- Privately purchased lists.

Practice Profiles

A practice profile provides information about a professional or group with whom you want to develop or have developed a relationship. You may use it to receive referrals and to send referrals. You can start this kind of profile with your Resource Directory Worksheet (Figure 6.2) and expand it as you have more contacts. The more you know about a business, the easier it is to send effective marketing pieces. You can sort your practice profiles by any field you set up in your database for easy access to the information you need for marketing or referral purposes. The data fields I recommend are:

- Name.
- Address.

Figure 6.11

Master Mailing Schedule

Master Mailing Schedule for Month of ___________

Date	What Sent	Target Population	Quantity	Cost
1.				
2.				
3.				
4.				
5.				
6.				
7.				
8.				
9.				
10.				
.				
.				
.				
31.				

- Telephone.
- Office hours.
- Mutual contacts.
- Mutual interests.
- Type of practice/specialty.
- Size of practice.
- Professional training and background.
- Orientation and attitudes toward psychotherapy.
- Professional contacts and resources.
- Standing and acceptance in professional community.
- Personal orientation and attitudes.
- Personal interests and involvements.
- Other important information.
- Dates of contacts.

Contact Planning Schedule

When you want to develop any particular contact, you can start a more detailed database. I include the following fields in my contact database:

- Name.
- Address.
- Telephone.
- Date of initial contact.
- Method of initial contact.
- Response.
- Planned date of follow-up.
- Planned method of follow-up.

Direct-mail marketing is an easy way to begin your marketing outreach. It is usually less threatening to the novice marketer and easy to track in terms of ROI. Be careful not to get stuck doing only direct mail. It has its place but is only one piece of your marketing mix.

ADVERTISING

Advertising can be very expensive, so it is important you know what you are doing. One of the most commonly used advertising formats used by psychotherapists is the yellow pages ad, which will be covered in detail in this section. When used correctly, advertising can support the growth of your business. The key is to be clear about the niche you are reaching out to and be consistent in your advertising efforts. You also need to think about the type of response you want from your advertising. Are you looking for:

- *Image Development.* Builds up, through repetition, a favorable impression of your service or product.
- *Increased Awareness.* Helps people remember something special about you. This could be your USP (unique selling principle).
- *News Interest.* Announces a workshop, new service or product, new location, or special event.
- *Promotions.* Encourages individuals in your target market to take some action that will lead to bringing them in as clients (e.g., a free screening for depression or stress).
- *Psychoeducation.* Often used by professionals. One block of the informative material describes their services or product and provides their name and address. This kind of ad presents you as a user-friendly expert in your arena.

- *Inquiry.* Invites inquiries that can be responded to with a newsletter, free audiotape, or information packet.
- *Database Building.* A method for acquiring names and addresses of people who are interested in your services to use later with a more intensive ad piece. A return postcard and an 800-number are good vehicles for this type of advertising.
- *Direct Order.* You may have created a book, audio- or videotape product and want to sell it. The ad is simple and to the point listing benefits of the product with an easy ordering process.

These ads can be combined, but it is best to be clear about the response you are soliciting; don't confuse your market with too many requests. Don't expect someone to order your book, register on your mailing list, send for an information packet, and sign up for a free screening all at the same time. Decide what is most important. You can do ads sequentially in the order determined by your marketing plan. Figure 6.12 lists some of the good and bad news about advertising.

Before you spend any money on advertising, make a plan. I can't think of an easier way to waste money than to begin a random advertising campaign or to place one ad and not follow through. Your resource database will help you identify the most strategic places to place your advertisements. The key questions are:

- What niche are you providing products or services to?
- What are your specialties and who will be interested in you?

You must answer these questions before you can design your ads and place them effectively. Professionals frequently ask me, "Where can I advertise that is ethical and tasteful?" I always suggest exploring the yellow pages first since

Figure 6.12

Advertising Pros and Cons

Advantages	Disadvantages
General Advertising	
Can produce immediate results in terms of calls for information or appointments.	Can be expensive and need to be repeated a number of times at great cost.
Can create a new demand for your services.	If not targeted well, can be a waste of money.
Reminds people that you are available.	Expensive form of marketing.

such directories seem to be the most acceptable medium in the profession (see Figure 6.13).

Yellow Pages Advertising

Successful advertising in the yellow pages is not a given. I know a professional whose specialty is sex therapy and who has positioned herself as an expert in her field. She lives in a region that is conservative and traditional; sex is not an open topic. She has chosen to take only word-of-mouth referrals and does not advertise in the yellow pages. Most of her advertising is done through networking and presentations to professionals about her specialty. Early in her career when she did advertise in the yellow pages, she found that the majority of her contacts were crank callers. Her business has flourished with the absence of a yellow page ad, and she no longer gets those annoying calls.

One of the first things to do if you decide to use the yellow pages is contact the company's representative and request an information packet. I recently received a typical packet with sample pages of my specialty from the surrounding areas. I could see what others were presenting in terms of graphics, text, and size of ad. The packet also included figures on responses to each ad.

After completing this research, call the people who have placed the ads and ask them how their advertisements are performing for them. Do the ads bring in the kinds of clients they want to have in their practice? This is an important step since yellow pages advertising is a regional phenomenon. What works in one region is not the same in another. Look at the ads that are getting responses and model your ad after them. To obtain your final design, you can work with the yellow pages consultant or create your own with another designer. When creating your ad:

- Don't include anything that will change over the year.
- Make sure your telephone number is easy to find and read.
- Include your logo if you have one.

Figure 6.13

Yellow Pages Advertising

Advantages	Disadvantages
Can be inexpensive in rural areas.	Can be expensive in cities.
Can bring in a lot of calls.	Time wasted answering many calls that do not result in new customers or clients.
A consistent ad will let people know you are still around and available.	Will need to change ad over time and that can be costly.

- Leave some white space; don't use a lot of text or a tiny typeface.
- Include any benefits you can offer:

  Insurance welcome.

  Sliding scale.

  Immediate appointments.

  Weekend/evening appointments.

  Wheelchair accessible.

  Parking available.

Responding to Yellow Pages Callers

Most people who use the yellow pages to access counseling services are seeking immediate care. You need to respond to them as soon as possible. If you rely on the yellow pages for referrals, I recommend that you wear a pager and return calls promptly.

Block Ads

Block ads are advertisements framed in a box. You see them in:

- Magazines.
- Journals.
- Newsletters.
- Periodicals.

Some of the points to remember in creating yellow pages ads also apply to block ads. Block ads can be expensive but cost less than a direct-mail piece. The following guidelines are helpful for creating block ads:

- Maintain a graphic identity that makes your ads easily recognizable wherever they run.
- Use a simple layout:

  Don't use many different type fonts.

  Don't use overelaborate borders.
- Use a dominant element such as a large picture, a headline, or a logo.
- Include a prominent benefit headline that immediately answers your targeted customer's presumed question: *Why would I be interested?*
- Let white space enhance your ad. Don't crowd information.
- Urge and direct customers to act now. Use words like call, register, or limited seating, to get them moving.
- Make certain to provide your signature or information about your business at the bottom where most everyone looks. Include your name, address, telephone and fax numbers, and e-mail address.

The keys to successful advertisements are:

- A dominant focal center to attract the reader's attention.
- A challenge to curiosity, an enticement to self-interest, or a promise to meet an important need.

Keep a file of ads that impress you and ones you have responded to. You can use them for models when you are ready to create your own.

Advertising can be expensive. It is important to choose your advertising vehicles strategically. To do this, you need to know:

- The characteristics of your ideal customer.
- Your services and your competition.
- The media that reach your ideal customer.

- Methods for creating effective advertising copy.

Before making a final decision about an ad, show it to colleagues and friends to get their opinions. Once you have produced it, keep running the ad consistently; don't change it too frequently. You want your reader to see you over and over again and remember who you are. Carefully designed and executed advertising pays off in the long run. When you find a vehicle or publication that brings you the business you want, you have struck gold. Use it wisely.

7

GETTING THE WORD OUT

Publicity and Promotion

Public Relations

Have you ever watched other professionals enthusiastically promote their services and wonder how they did it with such ease? When you read an article in a publication by a colleague, or about a colleague, does your perception of the person shift? You are being affected by public relations, which supports and enhances other marketing activities. Advertising and direct mail can be confused with public relations, but publicity is not advertising. Public relations or publicity can promote your business with a lower financial cost than advertising.

Once you have overcome the beginning hurdles of marketing and advertising, it is time to move into self-promotion. Unless no fear arises when you imagine telling everyone about your work, start small and work your way up to more difficult experiences. Even if you enjoy public speaking and self-promotion, this chapter will help you streamline and optimize your efforts. The following sections are presented developmentally, each one preparing you for championship self-promotion:

- Packaging.
- Professional associations.
- Authoring.
- Going electronic.
- Networking.
- Public speaking.
- Planned events.
- Using the media.

Packaging

Packaging is the first step in self-promotion. Packaging is what prompts you to buy new items in the supermarket. Like it or not, packaging is also what people see when they look at you, your office, your outreach brochures, and your professional presentations. Each image creates an immediate representation of who you are and determines how you are positioned in others' minds. Packaging can suggest an intangible quality that produces tangible results.

It is better to gain some control over how you are perceived than to allow a "whatever they want to think is okay" attitude jeopardize your position. If you want to take control over your future, you must consciously create a representation of who you are and what you do. Start with the arenas you already have in place and work your way out. Consider how you will design or redesign:

- Your office.
- Your wardrobe and accessories.
- Your business stationery.
- Your brochures.

Is there a central theme? Do you want to be seen as creative, traditional, Jungian? If you don't have any idea what your *packaging* identity is, it is time to find out. Grab a camera and start taking pictures. Have someone take a picture of you wearing your usual outfit for a business day. Take a picture of your office, your car, and your briefcase. Take these pictures and spread them out on the floor alongside your business stationery brochures. What do you see? Who is this person? What do you think about them? If you still don't get an idea about a central theme, ask a friend who will be honest. If all these things have some kind of unifying thread and you like the image, you're in great shape. If you believe something is missing or needs to change, start a design guide. This resembles a scrapbook but instead of personal mementos it contains pictures, articles, or any other business and professional representations that you like or are drawn to. Start looking at magazines you feel aligned with and cut out pictures of anything that attracts your eye or attention. Put them in your design guide. Certain themes will emerge to give you a sense of your own preferences. Once you have gathered several items you like, share these pictures with your friends and ask them what they think. Would this kind of image fit you? What you are looking for is an image, or package, you feel at home with. It is the totality of what others translate into who you are and how you are positioned. The interactive process is vital. You must know how others perceive your presentation. Video and audio feedback also are helpful. If you don't have any public events to tape, set up the recorder at home during a family event or even at mealtime. You want to know how you present yourself in public. You will act differently at home than you do in the business arena, but if home is all you have, use it. Your identity stamp is also in your telephone message or answering machine message; it precedes you when you walk in to a room; it speaks through your electronic home page. You want consistency and an awareness of what you are communicating every time. Now that your self-presentation has been addressed, it is time to go out in public.

Professional Associations

Working with your regional or national professional association provides an excellent opportunity for self-promotion. You can volunteer to sit on the board, join a committee, write articles for the newsletter or journal, or help at planned events. Not only are you promoting yourself and networking with other professionals in your area, you are promoting your profession—a win-win situation. If you don't agree with the direction your association is going, then get involved and help create change. Be careful not to get railroaded into doing busy work or unrewarding tasks. Ask yourself what you are good at and what you want to do. Then determine where these skills can be useful in the organization. I have not found a professional association yet that does not need volunteer help but take care to match your talents with its needs. Once you get involved, you will find more things to do than you have time for, so be sure to set limits on your involvement. Decide how many hours a month you are willing to volunteer and stand firm. It is better to follow through on your commitments than to overextend your obligations.

AUTHORING

Authoring includes everything you write or create in the verbal or visual media. Authoring is an excellent way for the more internal personality to become visible. Unlike extemporaneous speaking engagements, writing gives you time to create and arrange your thoughts before presenting them to the public. Figure 7.1 presents the pros and cons of authoring.

Professional Educational Literature

A good way to start is with short articles and information brochures. Such pieces can serve many purposes:

- To inform professionals about psychology and psychotherapy as they relate to their discipline.
- To educate and train professionals in specific techniques that can enhance their practices.
- To provide medical practitioners with materials that can help their patients (e.g., "Coping with the Idea of Surgery").

Patient Education Literature

Patient education literature helps clients help themselves with specific techniques and ideas on issues such as how to stop being a negative parent and start enjoying your children. The information brochure is an excellent vehicle for clients. The how-to article is an expanded version of the informational brochure.

How-to Articles

Think about writing a how-to article that is directly related to your experience or expertise and is relevant to the subject about which you want to be considered an expert. These articles are different from the psychoeducational materials in that they are more activity oriented. For example, you could describe how to:

- Run a family meeting.
- Set up a reward system for your children.
- Increase your self-esteem.
- Speak assertively.
- Get along with your (boss, partner, children, dog, or cat).

Once you have written your piece, you may ask "Now what?" Many resources at the library can provide guidance in finding a publisher. A book I have found valuable is *Writer's Market* (Garvey,

Figure 7.1

Authoring Pros and Cons

Advantages	Disadvantages
For the marketing phobic, writing is a way to avoid one-on-one marketing.	You can rely too heavily on the written word and never use any other kind of marketing tool.
Written articles and books help secure your position as an expert in your field.	If your work is not well thought out and edited, it can secure a position in the field you would rather not hold.
Writing can force you to put your thoughts into words so others can benefit from your education and experience.	Writing is time consuming.

1993). It includes basic information on writing and a list of categories of interest and the publications that feature such subject matter. Ask yourself if you know anyone who works for a publisher or a press. Do you know anyone who knows anyone with access to newspaper or magazine reporters, editors, or writers? Create a contact list with their names, addresses, and phone numbers; then call, write, and follow up. Be persistent, polite, and determined. When dealing with the media, perseverance often leads to success.

I believe writing about what you do is one of the best ways to promote your services. It has a twofold benefit: First, it forces you to put your thoughts into words so others can understand you; and second, it reaches more than that one person you see in a session. Your market expands and you benefit from the exercise—a true win-win approach to marketing.

GOING ELECTRONIC

To "go electronic," you need a computer. If you intend to use it for business, you need one dedicated for that purpose. Once you begin to discover the computer's capabilities, you will expand your uses and you will not want other people's files or limited access to impede your work. If you do not own one already, there are some things to think about before you rush out and buy one. If you are still pondering whether to buy one, stop now and just say yes. Then go on to the following questions about your requirements:

- What do you want to use the computer for? Look at the different options that follow in this chapter and decide which ones you are interested in.
- Is this part of a long-term strategy or single-purpose purchase? Will you be networking several offices or only using it for your individual needs?
- Do you have software in mind that you want to use?
- Do you want a World Wide Web presence?

Before you buy, you will need to decide:

- What platform you want to commit to, a DOS operating system or a Macintosh operating system.
- How much disc space and memory to include.
- What kind of modem to use.
- What kind of monitor to purchase.

Many computers come *bundled* with preselected hardware and software, but these may not provide the best solution for your needs. Be informed before you purchase because once you commit, it can be difficult to change. Unless you are knowledgeable about computers, consult someone whose judgment you trust. If you don't know anyone with the required expertise, ask your friends if they can recommend a qualified person. If you still come up empty, call the computer companies, they all provide referral services to consultants. The most important point is to clarify your use needs before you buy. Don't buy and have to adapt to imposed features of the hardware and software.

Here are some uses for your computer.

Electronic Mail

Electronic mail (e-mail) refers to the transmission of information on your computer through your modem. This piece of equipment processes the information coming out of your computer and sends it to a recipient computer through the telephone line. The modem then receives information coming back through the telephone line and sends it into your computer. It is a gateway. Information arrives through a public server like AOL (America On Line), or CompuServe, directly through the Internet, or via other computers you are *networked* with. Rather than write a letter and drop it in the mail, you create a letter on your computer and send it out through your modem to its receiver. It arrives instantly. Hence the new reference to traditional mail as *snail mail.* Some organizations now only communicate through electronic mail. You will be on the cutting edge when you can receive your own.

Internet

The Internet (Net) was created by the government and academia. Originally, computer experts (hackers) developed it to exchange and store information. It has become public through their creativity, and users can communicate on it without resorting to a centralized service. Since it is not centralized, no one can control it, which has its upside and its downside. For those of us who are not hackers, software programs such as Mosaic® and Netscape® are available. These programs overlay the complex network system, and users can access the Net by subscribing to a local server (e.g., TV cable or telephone). Our local service charges $30 per month and includes 60 hours of connect time.

This includes the Mosaic software, and 5 megabytes of space on their computer so we can create a home page for Lawless & Company.

Home Page

The Internet connects many locations, or sites, which are often referred to collectively as the World Wide Web. The home page or Web page is a place, or document, where people on the Web discover who you are. With Web page, you can:

- Attract business or offer services.
- Share special knowledge.
- Provide specific answers to queries.
- Connect with others of similar interests.
- Keep customers up to date on professional services and products.
- Reach the whole world.

The World Wide Web is a global medium, and your Web page is the contact everyone has with you. It is not a paper page but an interactive display of information you design. Your professional Web page is a marketing tool. It is also a networking tool. Your Web page can direct people to other Web pages for information related to yours. There are consultants who will set up a Web page for you; the consultant I use is SpeckTech, whose Internet address is "http://www.shore.net/~speckert." Their Web page includes text, pictures, and movies and is a good example of their work. *The Web Page Design Cookbook* (Horton, Taylor, Ignacio, & Hoft, 1996) is an excellent book on creating your own Web page and includes a CD-ROM to help you get started.

Computer Networks

A computer network is a group of electronically connected computers. They can transfer information back and forth, using software applications and other peripherals such as printers. These systems can be in-house or external. You can be networked with users in England. Your company could be networked with writers, editors, or anyone you want to receive or exchange information with. The networking can take place in real time, or one computer can be the server and handle information while other people's computers are turned off.

Videoconferencing

Videoconferencing occurs when people at various locations are taped by a video camera and these images are integrated into a single picture and sound medium. To set this up for yourself is very costly, but the Kinko's organization now has this service available at many of its locations. If you use this kind of linkup you can cut down on travel and hotel costs for meetings.

You can use your computer for other business purposes:

- Maintaining a database for your mailing lists.
- Keeping practice profiles.
- Managing your money.
- Managing your practice in terms of billing, record keeping, and tracking client visits.
- Desktop publishing, such as making your own advertisements and layouts for ads and newsletters or other promotional materials.
- Mail-merging your database into letters or documents that you send to many people.

- Creating mailing labels.
- Accessing research sites through the Internet.

The list can go on and on. I don't know how I operated before I went electronic. Don't ponder, just do it.

NETWORKING

Networking as a Business Skill

You have been networking all your life; now you can use this skill to develop your practice. Networking is the art of tapping the market of *people resources*. Meeting people who can help you develop your practice is interactive: You will need to give as much as you get in the exchange of information. Networking serves you in many ways. It can:

- Provide information for market research.
- Provide names of referral sources.
- Help you gain confidence in your self-presentation skills.
- Enable you to make new friends and find professional colleagues.

Through networking, I have made friends and met colleagues with whom I later developed joint business ventures.

Did you know that a referral is 80 percent more likely to create new business than a cold call? The referrals you receive through networking are the kind you want to have. It is said that the person you are looking for is three to five people away from you when you begin your search through networking. Like any other achievement, successful networking requires a plan for reaching specific goals. You can spend a lot of time going to meetings and gatherings, so you need to target where to put your time. Before you get started, answer the questions and make the assessments presented in Figure 7.2.

Individual Contacts

When you want to meet with an individual, you can send a letter or give the person a call, or both. You can ask to speak with him or her for a few minutes over the phone or suggest you meet for lunch. You can also ask for time to do an informational interview. Each person you network with will be a resource for new contacts. Always ask for the names of others who can help you in your networking goal. Be sure to ask how you can help the person you are speaking with. A simple telephone script goes something like this:

> Hello [respondent's name], my name is [your name] and I was given your name by [name of referral] as someone who can probably help me. I am talking to professionals in your area of [name of area] to gather more information. Could we [get together, schedule a telephone interview] for fifteen to twenty minutes?

Remember, the worst the person can say is no, and he or she may even enjoy sharing expertise with you.

Business or Group Gatherings

Remember to obey the following rules of etiquette for networking:

- Arrive on time.
- Do not smoke.
- Reintroduce yourself to people you know.

Figure 7.2

Networking Worksheet

Ask yourself:

- What do I want to gain from networking?
- What is my deadline for reaching my goal?

Next, assess your networking skills. The skills you need are:

- Presenting yourself in a positive way.
- Asking open-ended questions.
- Listening to metamessages.
- Showing interest in others.

(A good sense of humor also is a great asset in any social gathering.)
Where do you start? List everyone you know in the following areas:

- Informal contacts:
  Relatives.
  Friends.
  Neighbors.
  Social or club acquaintances (health club, professional associations, etc.).
  People you meet in your daily activities (bank tellers, garage mechanics, shopkeepers, etc.).
- Educational contacts:
  People you went to school with.
  Parents of your children's friends.
  Teachers, professors, and trainers you have met.

(Continued)

Figure 7.2 *(Continued)*

- Formal contacts:

  Colleagues.

  Consultants.

  Other professionals (lawyers, doctors, dentists, etc.).

  Hairdressers, manicurists, masseuses.

Next, go to the library and research the business journals and industry-specific publications related to your networking goals. With all this information in front of you, it is time to prioritize where to put your time.

- Exchange business cards only after a conversation in which you've initiated a relationship with the person.
- Do what you say you will do.
- Approach only groups of three or more.
- Learn the correct procedures for introductions.
- Don't flirt.
- Use humor but never at anyone else's expense; also avoid off-color jokes.
- Listen well.
- Don't monopolize either the buffet table or another person's attention.
- Make good eye contact and don't look at others while someone is talking to you.

Take a small notepad to jot down information. When someone gives you a business card, write down the date and place where you received it. Make sure you have a plentiful supply of business cards with you to hand out.

When you get home or back to your office, enter the information in your database in the appropriate categories. Follow up your meeting with any marketing materials that the new contacts might be interested in. If nothing seems appropriate, a simple note saying how you enjoyed meeting the person will suffice.

I suggest you make networking a habit. A good book for further reading on the topic is *Networking* (Clark, 1993).

PUBLIC SPEAKING

Public speaking has been one of those things people fear more than death. Most of us get butterflies, or worse when we know we are going to speak to an audience. Since I was identified as the shyest student in my high school, I intimately understand people's fears. The first time I gave a presentation to an audience (the Chamber of Commerce), my daughter came and sat in the audience. She was just graduating from a communications program in college, and I asked her to give me feedback on my performance. When I was through, and we were going over the evening, she asked me tactfully if I would consider taking a public speaking course, soon. She helped me realize I did not have the skills to get my information across. If I wanted any kind of follow-up business, I needed to learn how to motivate others to act. I took her advice and registered for a public speaking class at the local junior college and joined Toastmasters.® I must say the class was good, but I really learned more at Toastmasters. I cannot recommend them highly enough. They are a national group that provides structured learning experiences for both the beginning speaker and the more experienced speaker. They will send you a list of the Toastmaster groups in your area. Call them at 714-858-8255. Start now if you want to begin your speaking career.

There are more speaking opportunities than just formal presentations. Every time you tell someone about what you do, you are speaking. I have a self-presentation formula I teach people to use in my marketing workshops. It helps them get their message across while still being human. It also forces you to organize your thinking so you speak clearly and succinctly. Use this formula (described in the following section) and create a one- to three-minute *marketing script* for yourself.

When you create your marketing script, you must frame it to match your listeners' interests or your identified market. You would say something different to your neighbor or the local pastor than you would to a colleague.

The Marketing Script

Who You Are

This includes information about who you are in relationship to the service or product you are offering. Use language listeners will understand.

What You Do

Make this as concrete as possible. The abstract information can be talked about later when you have connected and are conversing with each other.

Why You Do It

This is as important for you as it is for them. For your customers, you are building a link between yourself and your offerings by explaining how they will benefit from what you are offering. Describe two or three clear benefits for them, but don't go overboard; your speech will just become confusing. For yourself, always ask yourself:

- Is this what I want to do?
- Is it congruent with who I am?

Why Your Listeners Might Be Interested in What You Are Offering

Now is the time to make the link between you and them. Perhaps there is none. If not, ask about anyone they know who might be interested. If you have done all the preceding steps well, people have a clear understanding about what you are offering. If you don't know how they might be interested, ask them if they are and if they are, why. If they are not interested, remember to ask why not.

How You Might Work Together in the Future

If the link has been made, people need to know what to do next. You need to design many ways for them to take the next step, ranging from an easy, simple, no-commitment inquiry to a jump-right-in-and-go-for-it contract with fiscal issues clarified. Do your homework first. Then you will be ready for every reaction.

Write a long and a short version. If writing is difficult for you, tape-record yourself telling a friend or colleague. Start someplace. If it is mumbling in the shower, fine. To get you going, I've included samples based on my own marketing scripts (see Figure 7.3).

After you have your marketing script, give your presentations to friends and trusted colleagues. After you give your short presentation, ask them for feedback about what they remember and what was most important to them. Remember, marketing is interactive. You need to listen to what people hear. You may find what you thought was a minor point was the only thing they remember. Ask them:

- What did you hear me say?
- What did I offer?
- What did you find the most interesting about my offering?
- Did my offer interest you overall:

  If yes—how?
  If no—why not?

Figure 7.3

Scripts Targeted to Specific Markets

Target Market: Professional Currently in or Considering Private Practice

Service: Practice Consultation

General Presentation at a Networking Event—Long Version

Hello, my name is Susan Froid. I am a licensed psychotherapist and professional practice consultant. I have been in private practice for over 12 years and have worked in the mental health field in a variety of settings for over 20 years. I consult with mental health professionals who are either in, or considering going into, professional practice. I help professionals set up office systems, optimize their business management, and promote their practice. It is important to me to help professionals develop and grow personally in their work. Together, we seek life balance, so they don't burn out and can continue to be a resource to their families and their community. I consult with professionals individually, lead working groups, and provide training for larger groups. I can be reached by telephone, fax, or E-mail. Here is my brochure describing my services in more detail. Please feel free to contact me with any questions you have about my services. (165 words)

Short Version

Hello, my name is Susan Froid. I am a Professional Practice Consultant. I help professionals set up, manage, and promote their professional practices. Working together, we address the individual and business developmental needs that arise as practitioners grow and expand their business. It is important to me to help psychotherapists maintain their personal wellness while growing their business. My services are personalized to meet the needs of the psychotherapist at any point in their development. I can be reached by telephone, fax, or E-mail. Here is my card. Please feel free to contact me with any questions you have about my service. (103 words)

(Continued)

Figure 7.3 *(Continued)*

Expanded Version

Hello, my name is Susan Froid. I am a licensed psychotherapist and a professional practice consultant. I have loved my work since I was a small child and enjoyed playing office more than playing with dolls. Professionally, I started working in aerospace as a methods analyst where I went into work settings and analyzed how work was accomplished. My task there was to optimize effort as well as paper and information flow, and create a more productive business system. Later, I worked in psychiatric hospitals that had to conform to accreditation standards for mental health settings. I worked my way up from the treatment level to become Team Leader and Program Manager. Simultaneously, I taught treatment techniques in academic settings. After leaving the hospital setting, I started several counseling practices. A group of friends and I set up a nonprofit group that evolved into a for-profit community based counseling center. More recently, I relocated to Boston where I started a private practice and created a group without walls with several colleagues. As I moved through all these arenas, I found it natural to create training materials while watching my personal process in the growth of my professional practice. My training and consultation work now offers the pragmatics of business and addresses the individual and business developmental process that evolves as the practitioner grows and the business expands. I help practitioners work within and outside the managed care arena.

Since I have experienced, and observed, how the mental health business can be a danger to practitioners' well-being, I have a firm commitment to helping counselors maintain their personal wellness while managing and growing their professional practices.

Where do you work now?
Are you in or have you considered starting a private practice?
How has it been going for you?
What challenges do you face today?

Private Practice Development training and consultation might be what can help you move to the next stage of your professional practice development. As a consultant, I teach and consult with individuals and groups. What I find works best is to consult individually and then form small working groups that deal with the personal process in the business development while providing ongoing support for this difficult endeavor.

(Continued)

Figure 7.3 *(Continued)*

If you are interested in any of these services, please give me a call to chat or set up an informational consultation to assess your current needs. Here is my card and a brochure. Please feel free to contact me with any questions you have. (417 words)

Target Market: Possible Referring Professional
Services: Psychotherapy

Hello, my name is Susan Froid. I am a Licensed Marriage Family Therapist and have been in private practice for over 12 years. I have worked in the mental health field in a variety of setting for over 20 years.

I counsel women who have been victimized in some physical or psychological way or have suffered a major loss such as a loved one, job loss, or any other loss that has affected them in a powerful way. Common symptoms I often see in new clients are eating disorders, depression, lack of a clear sense of self and low self-esteem, involvement in destructive relationships, work problems, and struggles with the family of origin.

I have found over the years that the women I work with become empowered and begin to hear and honor their inner wisdom. I seem to be able to help them discover their courage and honor and support how they want to live their life. I enjoy the process of reframing life traumas into a story of the heroine who learns valuable life lessons and finds the wisdom and courage to live a happy, healthy life.

Here is my card; please feel free to contact me to discuss my specialties. Please send me information about your practice for my referral source list. (221 words)

Target Market: General Public
Services: Psychotherapy

Hello, my name is Susan Froid. I am a psychotherapist with a private practice in Boston near Copley Plaza. My specialty is women's issues. I help women heal from psychological wounds they received as a child or an adult. Some of the symptoms I see in the women who come to me are problems with food and weight, fear of being themselves, shyness, depression, problems in the workplace, or difficulty dealing with a life change such as divorce or death of a loved one.

(Continued)

Figure 7.3 *(Continued)*

My personal experience as a woman in our American culture is that I have had to educate myself and learn how to create a new definition of a healthy empowered woman. I have had to create a definition that sets well on my heart and works at home and in the office. I follow the research done about how women change and grow into healthy people.

If you should ever want to contact me for any reason, I am available by telephone and offer low-fee individual consultations to help clients figure out what services are needed and who can best apply them. Here is my card, and I am listed in the Boston telephone book under Counseling. (202 words)

Target Market: Funeral Directors
Services: Psychotherapy—Bereavement

Hello, my name is Susan Froid. I am a Licensed Marriage Family Therapist in private practice for over 12 years. I have worked in the mental health field in a variety of settings for over 20 years. My office, near Copley Plaza in Boston, is easily accessible by public transportation. I am also wheelchair accessible and parking is safe in the nearby parking garage.

I work with individuals and families who have suffered the death of a loved one and help them through the process of grieving their loss.

I have suffered the loss of loved ones in my own life and have personal as well as clinical experience in healing through the grieving process.

You probably see many families who are in a lot of pain in your line of work. In fact, you might often be on the receiving end of their anger and frustration. Since that is part of the grieving process, you might consider providing them with resources that can help them work through the pain. I'm sure they will remember that you helped them with more than the funeral arrangements.

I am available for a free consultation to help people decide which resources will be in their best interest. Also, if you should ever have any questions about my work please feel free to give me a call or make an appointment to stop by.

Here are some of my cards and a brochure that tells you more about my work. Please feel free to call me for any reason. (257 words)

(Continued)

Figure 7.3 *(Continued)*

Target Market: General Public
Services: Training—Self-Management and Optimal Performance

Hello, my name is Susan Froid. I am a licensed counselor and professional consultant and trainer. I have been in private practice for over 12 years. I have worked in the human services arena in a variety of settings for over 20 years.

Out of my work with people over these years, I have developed a holistic self-management and personal organization system that I call LifeDance. LifeDance helps you create the life you want.

As a single working parent, I saw the need for a personal organization and self-management system in my own life while I was raising my daughter. I was challenged to create an integrated life that supported my personal health, a nurturing family base, and a career as a professional. As the years passed, I developed a system that seems to work and be easily learned and lived. I use it with clients who are ready for this challenge and teach the system to adults in individual and group settings.

How do you keep your life in order?
What life do you wish you had?

LifeDance can be a place to start and is also easily integrated with any other self-management system. LifeDance helps take people to their next level in personal health and life satisfaction.

Anybody can learn to use LifeDance and create more time to cultivate the skills they need for a healthier, more satisfying life. If you're interested in learning more about LifeDance, I can put you on my mailing list about upcoming workshops or we can get together to talk about a more personalized approach. If you know of a group who might like to know more about living healthier lives, have them call me. I offer lectures and work with organizations that might be interested in doing in-house training.

Here is my card and brochure. Please feel free to call me for any reason. (316 words)

- What would you do next in relationship to this offering?

You may be surprised about what they remembered. Use this technique on many individuals. Listen for patterns of responses. What do most of them remember? What do they not hear that is important to you?

With this information, you can begin to adjust how you present your offerings. Continue this dialogue for the rest of your marketing life. What you offer will change. How people hear you will also change because of the media flood we are all inundated with. Keep up the exchange.

Life presents one marketing opportunity after another. To optimize your progress, you need to consider what tools you want to use now and which ones you want to develop for the future. Here are a few ideas with some help in accomplishing them. I also suggest you use the many books and workshops that are available to expand your repertoire.

DONATING TIME

When you have the time, use it wisely. Many new practitioners who do not have their calendars filled with client hours have time to donate their services. At this point, your most important decision is where to offer your skills. The obvious answer is in an arena with the potential to bring business to your practice. I suggest getting to know an organization by making strategic, limited commitments to it. Then, when you find you enjoy working with them, and see yourself being reimbursed through connections with referral sources or direct referrals, decide how you want to maintain the relationship. When I was setting up a community counseling center, I donated time to a community group that was developing a human services directory. I didn't receive direct referrals but found it a great opportunity to meet the local professionals and other business leaders. After the directory was completed, I offered to maintain it with yearly updates. This kept me in touch with other referral resources and forced me to maintain my networking efforts. The group and I both benefited: The agency did not need to spend any money for its directory and I was able to network with referral sources in my community.

You can donate your time in any way. Some clinicians offer clinical services, others speak or provide training. The key is, don't waste your time or try to create a need when there isn't one. Look for win-win situations.

PLANNED EVENTS

Planned events are a good way to get noticed. The easiest planned event for most professionals is the opening of their new office or an open house. We held an open house when we opened our office in Benicia and met other professionals in the area and new referral sources. My partner's mother insisted on catering and my daughter helped decorate. We placed flyers in every business within a six-block radius and mailed them to all our friends and colleagues. Acquaintances we were certain would be there did not show up and people we didn't think would ever come showed. We chatted and handed out informational brochures all day long. It was especially busy around lunchtime. Some visitors hung around with us for a while. Others came in and out only to eat and leave us their card. You will find that the location of your office dictates how you advertise your open house. My current office is in a large building in downtown Boston. When I opened my office there, I left flyers in all the offices in the building and mailed them out to all my friends and colleagues. The turnout was similar to the one in Benicia, but many people stopped by primarily to market their services.

Other kinds of events are just as much fun as an open house. We ran a weekly video series for a couple months with a good turnout. We rented the Joseph Campbell video series from the local library and had a discussion after each film. Many media catalogs will let you rent films if you do not have the capital to buy. Many professional associations have a media series they offer free of charge. The American Psychiatric Association (APA) has a video series available on many diagnoses. We chose to go with a less clinical, more entertaining medium. I have colleagues who ran a "Shrink" series. They rented several movies that have a therapist as a main character, and afterward we talked about stigma in mental health. (The movie *What About Bob* was a favorite.)

You can also have reading groups and other discussion groups meet at your office, or you can offer a course on a problem like sexual harassment. All of these events will add to your visibility in your community. The wonderful thing about them is they are fun and usually free; however, they are also time consuming. The pros and cons of planned events are summarized in Figure 7.4.

MEDIA EXPOSURE

Just because your business is new or small, you may think you are not newsworthy, but this is not true. In fact, a story about an upcoming entrepreneur has more news value than the familiar corporate media outreach, no matter how professionally written.

To court media coverage most effectively, you need to understand that newspapers, magazines, newsletters, radio programs, and television news are all driven by common needs: to fill time and space, to be special, to be first, and to provide valuable information to readers, viewers, and listeners. Nothing in this list of basic requirements excludes new or small businesses.

From a journalist's perspective, a small business must rely on wit, enterprise, and ingenuity to survive, qualities that often make good stories. Not having received extensive media attention can be to your advantage since your ideas are new. Also, you are a real person instead of a carefully groomed corporate figure, which contributes to your attractiveness.

Gaining media attention is not an exact science, but there are some principles and practices that can guide your successful outreach efforts.

Consider the publications and programs you value. Look for media outlets that specifically serve your customers and clients. Consult the media guides that are available at bookstores, libraries, and publishers:

- *Directory of Experts, Authorities and Spokespersons,* Broadcast Interview Source, 2233 Wisconsin Avenue NW, Washington, DC 20007. Tel. 1-202-333-4904.
- *Bacon's Publicity Checker* lists more than 18,000 newspapers and magazines as well as 100,000 media contacts. Bacon Publishing Company, Inc., 332 South Michigan Avenue, Chicago, IL 60604. Tel. 1-800-621-0561.

Figure 7.4

Pros and Cons of Planned Events

Advantages	Disadvantages
Teaching provides a great opportunity for personal contact or public relations.	You need enthusiasm and showmanship to hold the attention of an audience.
You can become and be known as an expert in your area.	Marketing a workshop can be expensive.
Teaching in addition to a private practice can bring in new clients.	When old or current clients attend a workshop or event, you are faced with the issue of dual relationship.
Many adult education centers will do all the outreach for your class.	Preparing for and presenting a class can be time consuming.
An open house can bring in new contacts from your immediate area.	Planning for an open house can be time consuming.

- *Broadcasting Yearbook* covers radio, TV, and cable outlets in the United States and Canada and their staffs. Broadcasting Publications, Inc., 1705 DeSales Street NW, Washington, DC 20036. Tel. 1-800-638-7827.
- *Gale Directory of Publications* information regarding 25,000 newspapers, magazines, journals, and newsletters arranged by location. Gale Research Inc., 835 Penobscot Building, Detroit, MI 48266. Tel. 1-313-961-2242.
- *Hudson's Newsletter Directory* a listing of more than 4,000 subscription newsletters by subject. Also shows who wants news releases, photos, and so on. The Newsletter Clearinghouse, P.O. Box 311, Rhinebeck, NY 12572. Tel. 1-914-876-2081.

Although media contacts receive hundreds of news releases every day, the copy is often ineffective. Many are overtly self-serving and, because they are sent to many reporters, they lack exclusivity. When composing a news release, keep the following points in mind:

- Write about a topic, not about yourself.
- Be factual.
- Be brief: Limit the release to one page.

You may want to send the following items along with your news release:

- A cover letter that individually addresses the journalist or media person.
- A history of your business.
- A practice narrative.
- A brief autobiographical sketch including any publications you have written that relate to the topic.
- Anything else you have done that relates to the topic at hand. This could be a newsletter, a speech you have given, seminars or workshops, or articles published in other publications.

If you want extensive publicity, many talk-show producers and bookers locate speakers using the annual *Directory of Experts, Authorities and Spokespersons* (1995). This publication lists psychologists, feminists, astrologers, nutritionists, lawyers, association officers, union leaders, those who favor or oppose gun control, abortion, alcohol, animal rights, taxes, religion, and a litany of other topics. You can also be listed. The directory is distributed to 7,000 media outlets. If you decide to list yourself in this book, be ready for media coverage. (See Figure 7.5.)

GOING PUBLIC

Writing Your First Press Release

The basic tool for generating publicity is the news release document, which can secure free publicity from newspapers, magazines, radio, and television. Most of the news in newspapers and magazines comes from news releases sent

Figure 7.5

Pros and Cons of Media Coverage

Advantages	Disadvantages
An appearance in the media can enhance your credibility.	Being misquoted or having what you say taken out of context can be unflattering.
You may obtain referrals and inquiries about your services.	Responses can be sporadic and slow.
Radio and television exposure can be exciting; you can reach others who would never have known about you in any other way.	This kind of exposure may feed your ego but not your pocketbook. You may receive crank calls depending on your topic.

out by companies, government agencies, associations, individuals, and groups. The news release is an article written by you, about a topic:

- A public interest story about a current event.
- Response to pending legislation.
- Response to another news article.
- Response to a regional event.
- Addressing a social issue.

You cannot submit a press release about the good job you have done with your client who just terminated treatment, but ethical professionals can seek media coverage for many events:

- Opening a new office.
- Publishing anything.
- Learning a new technique.
- Adding a new partner to the office.
- Starting a public resource library in their office.
- Self-help groups.
- Attending an important conference.
- Creating reading groups on mental health topics.
- Holding workshops or speaking engagements.

Include the following information in your press release for each of the topic areas:

New Service Announcement

- Who you are.
- The primary services you offer.
- Secondary services and benefits to clients.
- Where your office is located.
- The need for your services.
- The benefits of your services.
- Your professional qualifications, positions held, or awards received.
- Your availability and how to contact you.

Program Announcement

- The type of program.
- When it is taking place.
- Where it is taking place.
- Cost (some people leave this out hoping consumers will call to find out).
- Benefits of the program.
- How to register.
- A brief statement about yourself and your business.

Feature Article

- Opening:

  Who you are.
- Body Text:

  The services or products you offer.

  The benefits of the services.

  The timeliness of the services.

  Who can use your services.

  The cost of your services.

  Where you are located.

  Some kind of quote validating the use of your kind of services.

  An industry analysis of your services' importance.

  Any warnings about using your services.

  Your position regarding your services.

- Closing:

  Your professional qualifications, positions held, or awards received.

  Your availability and how to contact you.

It is important to prepare your news release in the form the media wants to receive it. While some room for creativity exists, there is a common, easy-to-follow format you should follow. The release has several key elements: the originator (you), the release date, the contact, a headline, and the double-spaced copy itself. If you send out the news release on your business stationery, that will take care of the originator. All you have to do is type NEWS or NEWS RELEASE in capital letters at the top of the letterhead.

The release date is the date you want the story released. Usually, it can say "For Immediate Release." This is probably best, unless there is some reason for not releasing the story before a certain date. Also necessary is the name of a person to contact for further information. Along with the name, include the telephone number and area code where that person can be reached. If the material is extremely time-sensitive, you may want to include an evening phone number and FAX number along with the daytime number.

The headline should appear in capital letters, six spaces below the contact line. Sometimes called a *tickler,* it should be as clever and catchy as possible so it captures the attention and arouses the interest of the editor or producer. Newspaper headlines can be used as models of how to write news release headlines. Try for a headline that compels the reader to read the entire release.

Eight spaces below the headline, you should begin the body of the release. It should be double-spaced and written like a newspaper article, with the most important information in the first paragraph, the supporting information next, and the least important information last. Most people read the leading sentences to an article before they commit to reading more. You want to catch their attention right up front. A news release can be any length, but a one-page release probably has the best chance of being published. If you use more than one page, place the word "More" at the bottom center of the first page.

Because your release may be reprinted in its original form in some publications, spend enough time to compose well. Sometimes, your release may even be used as the basis for a feature story.

It's a good idea for your news releases to end with a "For more information" paragraph. Use this to give your company's name, address, and phone number and to offer a free informational brochure or some kind of promotional material. Doing this encourages people to contact your business, giving you new prospects and an opportunity to measure the impact of that particular coverage.

If you are particularly interested in developing a high media profile, you may also want to add a line at the bottom of your release saying *Media interviews welcome.* Professionals and others in personal service businesses can benefit most by being recognized as experts in their field by the media. You can also send a good black and white photograph of yourself. You never know when they might need filler and will use your picture.

Be sure to key each news release so you can identify the source of your inquiries. A simple keying system involves placing a department code somewhere in your address on the release (e.g., 123 Washington Street, Dept. ET). The code would identify a release sent to a specific publication (e.g., *The Boston Globe*). You could use numbers as codes instead of letters, or a combination. Figure 7.6 illustrates what the elements of a news release look like in actual use.

While sending out news releases is the most obvious part of getting mentioned in the media, identifying and creating real news about your product or service is the first step. Following that is identifying and contacting the appropriate media to receive your news release. To get the best results, send your news releases only to the media whose audiences are most likely to be interested in what you have to say. Most regions have some kind of media book. Check with nearby universities for this information, particularly if they have any kind of media or communications specialties. Ask your local librarian. It will save you a lot of time if you identify the regional media and their target audiences. Channeling your news releases to the right person is extremely important. Newspapers and magazines have specialized editors, while each radio and television talk show has a specific producer. Your best chance for getting the publicity you desire is by directing your release to the appropriate editor or producer. Always double-check your resources before you send anything out since media personnel turn over frequently.

Follow-up of media releases often gets overlooked, but it is crucial to any publicity campaign. Make follow-up phone calls to your media contacts to make sure they received your release. Don't try to pressure them into running your release, however; and if they don't run it, don't call and complain.

If you're convinced that your releases would be of interest to a particular audience, keep sending your contacts new releases and following up. The more releases you send, the more likely one of them will eventually be run. Don't get discouraged, just keep trying. If your releases are newsworthy, with enough patience and persistence, you'll get them placed. If you have been sending in releases and getting no response, call the editor or person you are trying to get a response from and ask why your pieces haven't appeared. Keep a record of who receives what, so you don't overlap or duplicate pieces in a small region.

The News Release Cover Letter

Unlike a news release, a letter can be personal, prepared and typed for an individual. As a rule, if you take the time to write thoughtfully to reporters, they will take the time to consider your ideas. I suggest you choose a few journalists to develop relationships with and send your press releases with cover letters like the one shown in Figure 7.7.

This letter is concise while conveying expertise and credibility. More importantly, the letter is not boastful, or demanding, in contrast to many of the letters journalists receive.

When you get a response to your publicity releases and are contacted by a media person for an interview, refer to the *Interview Subject's Bill of Rights.* You have the right:

- To know who is interviewing you and who he or she represents.
- To have total agreement by both parties about the ground rules.
- To be treated courteously.
- To have "off the record" comments honored when they are so identified.
- To know how long the interview will last.

Figure 7.6

News Release

Announcement—New Practice

NEWS RELEASE

For Immediate Release 1-1-97
Contact: Dr. Susan Froid 617-123-4567, Fax 617-123-7654

New Resource for Community

Dr. Susan Froid, Licensed Psychologist, Licensed Marriage & Family Therapist, and Certified Group Therapist announces the opening of her psychotherapy practice, Therapy Inc. The practice specializes in therapy and counseling for individuals, couples, and families in traditional and nontraditional situations with an emphasis on personal growth, inner development, personal relationships, and spiritual development.

Couples who are considering divorce can find new ways of communicating and help one another grow personally while strengthening their marriage. Families can learn to play and work together. Individuals, while eliminating destructive living habits, can begin to answer questions like *Who am I* and *What does my life mean?*

A Master's and Doctoral Degree in Clinical Psychology equip Dr. Froid to provide quality psychotherapy. Previously, Ms. Froid maintained a practice in New York. Her new office is conveniently located across from Copley Plaza in downtown Boston. Appointments can be made by calling 617-123-4567. An initial information interview is offered, at a reduced fee, to help you determine your needs and the best possible resources to help you.

(171 words)

(Continued)

Figure 7.6 *(Continued)*

Announcement—New Service

NEWS RELEASE

For Immediate Release 1-1-97
Contact: Dr. Susan Froid 617-123-4567

What Do Women Want?

METIS, a group for women in transition from divorce, career change, low self-esteem, or codependency, will be offered through Therapy, Inc. beginning 1-1-97.

Often the effects of major life changes, chronic low self-esteem, and life traumas create a devaluing of ones' sense of self. Many women experience depression and a general feeling of helplessness and frustration in life. The recovery of a woman's self-esteem and belief in herself is necessary to create a new future.

METIS, meaning wise counsel, is a therapy group designed to provide women a safe setting in which to explore the common difficulties they share. Often women's psychic wounds are woman-specific and are best facilitated in an all-female environment. The group meets once a week for two hours and each group lasts 10 weeks. The cost for each meeting is $45 and might be covered by health insurance.

Group facilitator Susan Froid is a licensed Psychologist and Marriage Family Therapist. She has been in private practice since 1983 and has worked in the mental health field for over 20 years. Ms. Froid holds three degrees in psychology and has led groups, and taught and directed psychiatric treatment teams. Her office is conveniently located across from Copley Plaza in downtown Boston. The office can be reached by public transportation. Safe parking is also available next door in the Copley parking garage.

For more information about METIS, or to register, call Dr. Froid's office at 617-123-4567.

(250 words)

Figure 7.7

Cover Letter

Dear ______,

In the past three years, the issue of family violence has become increasingly visible. Family violence leaves children homeless and often results in the death of family members. Family violence is as much a threat to health as cancer.

Since most families who are caught up in the violence cycle do not reach out for help, it is important that other family members and friends know the signs of violence in the behavior of children and the adults who are caught up in the cycle.

Your readers will want to know how family violence begins, how it goes out of control, and the five strategies to get out of the cycle. Family counselors are trained to help families get out of the cycle of violence. They can help educate the community to be an early warning system and support when families are trying to change. As a Licensed Family Child Counselor with 15 years' experience in this field, I hope you will feel free to call me for more information when you are writing about family violence.

Sincerely,

- To break off the interview within a reasonable amount of time after answering the important questions.
- To know whether other people will be interviewed about the topic and who they are, and if they will be present at the same time you are.
- To make sure no material is recorded by others without your approval.
- To have an accurate on-air introduction that will put your interview in the proper perspective.
- To have time to get some of your points across during the interview.

The following resources for marketing to the media may be available at your local library:

- *Literary Market Place* (New York: R. R. Bowker) a reference book updated annually. It lists television shows, radio shows, and newspapers of particular interest to authors.
- *Gale Directory of Publications and Broadcast Media* (Detroit: Gale Research) a directory of newspapers and media organized by states, listing potential media outlets.

THE DIALOGUE BETWEEN MARKETING, SELF-PROMOTION, AND PROFESSIONAL DEVELOPMENT

You must constantly ask yourself whether the direction your career is moving is congruent with who you are and what you want out of life. It is easy to get caught up in an expanding practice and lose track of how it is facilitating your personal and professional growth. If you find you no longer enjoy what you are doing, ask yourself if you can do it in another way. Delegate the tasks you dislike and take on the challenges you are drawn to. When you lose your passion for your work, you will reveal that loss in your diminished level of success and reduced value to the community.

8

MANAGING TO CARE

In the past 14 years, managed care organizations (MCOs) or behavioral healthcare organizations (BHOs) have dramatically changed the delivery of mental health care in the United States. The change has affected almost all individual practitioners by reducing their client load, and if they have chosen to work in the system, increasing paperwork, and decreasing fees paid for services. Most MCOs have also imposed a short-term, strategic treatment model and treatment review and evaluation on their providers. When I bring up the topic of managed care among my colleagues, it is similar to bringing up religion or politics. There are usually many strong feelings and often black-and-white thinking. The polarities are usually that one should either embrace managed care and learn to work with it or stay out of it completely. I believe each person must make this decision for his or her own reasons. Whether your reasons are pragmatic or philosophical, the decision—in any case—is yours. This chapter will give you options in both arenas, working within and outside the MCO system.

What Is Managed Care?

Confusion often arises when the phrase *managed care* is used among treatment specialists and the public. There is the broad-brush definition that encompasses all the companies and agencies that manage mental health benefits and the more specific breakdown of the different types of managed care entities such as HMOs (health maintenance organizations), PPOs (preferred provider organizations), and more. For this chapter's purposes, managed care means any system that contains utilization management, case management, provider selection, and cost containment.

Managed care is a system, not an entity. Members of this system are:

- Providers.
- Business, or the purchaser of the services.
- Consumers.
- National and regional laws.
- National and regional legislation.
- Managed care organizations.

For you to stay abreast of the managed care industry, you need to stay informed about changes in any part of the system.

The History of Managed Care

Managed care is not really a new concept. It has been around at least since 1300 and probably before then. The history of managed care is also the history of the biomedicalization of mental health. If the *Diagnostic and Statistical Manual of Mental Disorders* (*DSM;* American Psychiatric Association, 1994 [and earlier editions]) had not existed before managed care, those companies would have had to develop a system for categorizing mental illness. The *DSM* provides a means to equate dollar amounts to mental illness in much the same way as equating the cost of a broken leg to average procedures.

In the 1300s, Bernat de Berriac received 5 to 20 sous a year from each of several dozen men of modest means from Castello d'Empuries, a village in Catalonia. For this sum, he agreed to treat these men and their wives, children, and servants for "every illness that requires the art of medicine." He did not include dental work since that was covered by the barber. In the 14th century when the medical professional was just taking on an identity, physicians offered their services on retainer to royalty and the church. Many towns put a doctor on the payroll to cover the needs of the community. There has been a gradual transition from tribal unity, clan solidarity, family cohesion, the creation of guilds, and the concept of social welfare to today's marketplace. The following is a list of major milestones:

- *1883.* Emil Kraepelin published *The Compendium of Psychiatry* which systematized diagnostic groupings of mental disease.
- *1905.* Freud came to the United States and established psychotherapy under the domain of the medical practitioner. Only physicians could be trained to use his techniques. Psychiatry became a part of the mental hygiene movement.
- *1910.* The *Flexner Report* put stringent controls over medical education and licensure, eliminating homeopathy or osteopathy. Psychiatry became increasingly based on the biomedical, disease model, isolating problems and seeking to dominate them. Mental measures were used more frequently to determine the fitness for combat for soldiers and also for treatment of traumatized veterans.
- *1914.* With the Harrison Narcotic Act of 1914, home remedies and patent medicines gave way to physicians, hospitals, and pharmacists.
- *1917.* The Committee on Statistics of the American Psychiatric Association in collaboration with the National Commission on Mental Hygiene and the Bureau of the Census gathered uniform statistics from mental hospitals.
- *1952.* The first edition of the *Diagnostic and Statistical Manual of Mental Disorders* (DSM-1)
- *1930–1960.* Psychopharmacology emerged reducing the need for staffing and hospital

beds and emphasizing the biomedical nature of mental illness. Patients became accustomed to visiting the doctor and leaving with a prescription in hand. The prescription became the solution.

- *1960–1973.* State funded hospitals grew to house the mentally ill and developmentally disabled who could not be treated adequately in private settings.
- *1973 to Present.* Government has cut funding for mental health hospitals and funneled it toward privatization and community resources. Emphasis is placed on the psychosocial rehabilitation and raising levels of functionality.

In 1981, federal funding for HMOs was stopped and existing business scrambled for new ways to stay fiscally healthy. The privatization of health and mental health services began in earnest. This transition is often considered to have inaugurated managed care as we know it today.

From Art to Industry

Many professionals feel the change in their practice but do not know how to describe it. I find identifying the difference between practicing an art and working in an industrial setting a good comparison. Artists reach an outcome but cannot tell you how they got there. Workers in the automobile plant are following the procedures they were given to reach an outcome. Some professionals believe they can practice their art within the constraints of managed care, which has provided a structure for treatment or practice, or procedural guidelines. Others do not accept the intrusion of any external structure.

Managed care has forced the psychotherapy profession to identify how it facilitates healing or creates change. There has been closer scrutiny about what facilitates change and a clarification between addressing symptoms and causes. I am not concerned that the art of psychotherapy will be lost. There will always be those who practice and write about their art. The future will tell us whether that art can be contained within the industry.

How Can I Determine the Level of My Profession's Industrialization in My Region?

The industrialization of psychotherapy follows a predictable process. Look at the following stages and identify where your region stands today:

- *Stage 1.* Unstructured care is the norm; there is little managed care or hospital consolidation. The individual provider uses fee-for-service, indemnity plans, and some managed care.
- *Stage 2.* A loose framework begins to form in which most managed care consists of discounted fee-for-service care. Hospital consolidation begins, insurers begin to acquire or partner with providers, provider groups form, and an oversupply of mental health beds supports deep price discounts. The individual provider is often included in provider panels.
- *Stage 3.* Consolidation occurs with heavy managed care penetration into regional and government programs and also private plans. Managed care dominates as a payment source. Some capitation is used, hospital mergers and acquisitions take place, and

some plans begin dropping providers. As managed care consolidates itself, providers and insurers begin to align. The individual provider finds it more difficult to get a position on panels.

- *Stage 4.* Managed competition takes shape. Employer coalitions buy healthcare contracts and managed care payment dominates rather than fee-for-service. A few large healthcare players dominate the region. Providers and insurers are strongly aligned. Networks develop a full continuum of subacute care. Providers and insurers organize to serve covered lives. More than 50 percent of people insured use an HMO. The individual provider rarely can get on panels.

Phases of Managed Care

MCOs also go through phases of development. Consider the phase of development of any managed care company you are currently working for. Most MCOs today are in the third or fourth stage of development.

- *First Generation* reduces costs by restricting access to services through rigid utilization review, limited benefits, and large copayments.
- *Second Generation* begins the creation of provider networks, selective contracting, increased treatment planning, and less rigid utilization review.
- *Third Generation* manages the care of patients by emphasizing treatment planning and more active client management during treatment. It allows the use of the least restrictive treatment settings that are clinically appropriate.
- *Fourth Generation* manages by outcomes. Greater provider autonomy achieves successful outcomes by creating a self-correcting treatment system.

The Diversity of MCOs

MCOs cover many populations with varied benefits in different regions. They use separate eligibility criteria for consumers and providers, and have a wide range of utilization review procedures. The modes of delivery vary as well as their funding sources. Different professionals demand varying payment scales and treatment modalities. A nationwide coordinated design of treatment models, systems of delivery, and public policy does not exist. Power is widely dispersed between conflicting special interest groups, and regional needs vary greatly. At the same time, our population is growing older creating new resource needs for the population. Thus, "managed care" means different things to people depending on their region and type of experience.

Types of Insurance or Managed Care Entities

Commercial Carriers

Payments are made to qualified providers (or beneficiary) based on a schedule of benefits for specified services.

Fee-for-Service

A benefit package with no network direction consisting of a high degree of choice and flexibility such as Blue Cross/Blue Shield. It is an independent, not-for-profit, membership corporation providing protection against the cost of hospital or medical care. They are called prepayment plans because individuals pay in advance for the health services they may need. Providers are asked to complete an application and be preapproved although often out-of-panel providers are reimbursed at a lower percentage.

Self-Insured Welfare Plan

Benefits are provided directly by an employer or through an employee union or retirement plan such as the Retail Clerks Union Plan.

Health Maintenance Organization (HMO)

This is a staff model system in which providers are usually employed. Referrals are only made when a client requires services not provided in-house. Subscribers usually pay monthly premiums and often copayments at the time they receive services. Two examples are Kaiser Permanente and Harvard Community Health Plan.

Preferred Provider Organization (PPO)

This is a group of providers who have contractually agreed to provide services for a standard fee set by or negotiated with the managed care system. Usually subscribers have a deductible, pay an annual fee, and have some form of copay for services received. Examples are OHS Occupational Health Services and Value Behavioral Health, Inc.

Exclusive Provider Organization (EPO)

Although it resembles a PPO, the EPO is usually smaller allowing more control of the provider network. Generally, EPOs do not pay any percentage of out-of-panel provider services.

Employee Assistance Program (EAP)

This is an in-house or external system that assesses employees' needs. Some EAPs have in-house services but most refer to providers outside their system. The referral providers usually are noncontractual.

Point of Service

The employer offers different options to employees (e.g., a PPO, an HMO, an EPO, and an indemnity plan). There is generally a window of opportunity each year when employees can change the system they want to use.

Utilization Review Companies

Generally thought of as gatekeepers, these organizations review client needs and authorize the services they believe are necessary for treatment.

Medical Savings Account (MSA)

Employees have funds automatically deducted from their paycheck, pretaxable, and this account is used only for medical expenses.

Civilian Health and Medical Program of the Uniformed Services (CHAMPUS), Medicare, Medicaid

These government programs have their own list of acceptable participating providers. These systems are currently in the process of converting to an MCO model.

Workers' Compensation

These are benefits for employees who suffer injury or disability as a result of job-related accidents or occupational diseases. For a complete breakdown on workers' compensation laws for your state, write to the U.S. Chamber of Commerce, Publications Dept., 1615 H Street NW, Washington, DC 20062 (tel. 1-202-659-6000).

The Future of Managed Care

Since the behavioral healthcare marketplace is driven to meet the needs of customers, it will consist of a multiproduct framework. The market segments are predicted to be:

- *Fee-for-Service.* This is a premium product for highly paid employees who want the most flexibility and choice available to them. Employees and owners will have a pool of providers who have been identified by specialty services. There may or may not be a contractual agreement for reduced fees with the provider based on volume and availability.
- *Preferred Provider Organization.* This will be a traditional PPO as described earlier.
- *Exclusive Provider Organization or Health Maintenance Organization with a Point-of-Service Option.* This market segment will be made up of members willing to work with a gatekeeper and will retain the option of out-of-system benefits.
- *Basic Health Maintenance Organization.* This will be a pure HMO with the priority placed on cost savings rather than choice.

Behavioral healthcare companies will jockey to offer a full range of market segment choices and will create joint ventures to assure that they can cover as much of the marketplace as possible. They will loosen the strings on utilization review allowing more control for the providers in determining the need for visits (with a cap on number of visits or total monies allowed) and will choose to work with known group practices that have a history of good internal case management.

All of the following events have been predicted, and some of these changes are beginning to take place:

- An integration of employee assistance programs, managed behavioral products, and workers' compensation.
- Medicare moving to a managed care model.
- An integrated health data system for outcomes measures and provider performance ratings.
- Standardization of treatment methods, often called "practice standards." Many MCOs already provide these for their providers.
- More government regulation on the practices of all levels of managed care.

To Work, or Not to Work, in the Managed Care Marketplace?

This is often considered a black-and-white question—either you do or you don't. I believe there are several shades of gray. On one extreme is the individual provider who bases more than 50 percent of his or her client fees on managed care organizations. The other side of the scale is the provider who will take no managed care monies directly for any service. The gray areas include:

- The individual provider who limits MCO fees to 25 to 33 percent of client fees.

- The individual provider who works with a group that takes MCO payments.
- The individual provider who is part of a group that is offering an alternative to managed care and is competing for managed care contracts.
- The group that provides management support services (MSO) for clinicians but provides no client care.

Arguments against Working with Managed Care Organizations

If you choose to not include MCO clients in your practice you need to stay aware of the current trends in the marketplace. There are often opportunities to offer carve-out services, on your own terms, that are a good match with your skills. Carve-outs can be lucrative business opportunities. The individual practitioner who will do well outside managed care will be one who has used the business and marketing skills laid out in this book. Many practitioners market the benefits for clients who use their services without using their insurance. Some of these benefits are:

- The ability to choose whom they want to work with.
- More control over their treatment choices once they are in therapy.
- No fear about confidentiality.
- No record of mental health treatment in their insurance records.

There are groups forming that are positioned as *alternatives* to managed care. They are seeking to create a business model that does not divert large profits to stockholders and executives, reduces the administrative costs from 33 percent of the healthcare dollar to 10 percent or less, and operates collaboratively with its providers. The American Mental Health Alliance (AMHA) is one of these organizations. AMHA grew out of the National Coalition of Mental Health Professionals and Consumers (often called the Consortium), an advocacy organization that does not believe managed care is good for mental health. For more information about the Consortium, including whether there is a group in your region, and the growth of alliances in individual states, call the Consortium at 1-516-424-5232. They have many articles to inform providers and consumers about their beliefs and research. The AMHA seeks to put the care decisions back into the hands of the provider and client, support long-term treatment when necessary, and promote an organization that is responsive to the needs of the provider, the clients, and business. The mission statement of AMHA includes a commitment to quality, patients rights, privacy, and confidentiality. You can find out if there is an AMHA group in your region by contacting the Coalition at 1-516-424-5232.

Another group that has created an alternative to managed care for the provider and the consumer is the Boulder Psychotherapists Guild. The guild provides a member directory complete with a picture of each therapist, marketing and advertising for its members, and a newsletter describing groups and other activities offered by its professional members. The group will send you an information packet about its activities (tel. 1-303-444-1036).

Arguments for Working with Managed Care Organizations

If you are not currently working with a managed care company and have decided you want to get started, I suggest you sample working with one or two companies and then make an informed decision about pursuing this marketplace. If you decide to proceed, I believe it is foolish to base a practice primarily on managed care. The marketplace is changing too rapidly to place your professional fiscal future on managed care or any single referral source.

If you choose to work with MCOs, you need to make a good job of it. That means having your bookkeeping and record-keeping systems up to standard and staying on top of outpatient reports and treatment authorizations. With more effort going into provider "report cards" and a national database of providers, you do not want to enter the arena, do a sloppy job, and get a low rating that will affect choices you can make about future business. Another good reason is that managed care companies are shifting both general financial risks and professional liability risks to the providers. When you document all transactions between yourself and your client as well as the managed care company, you are in a much better position if any problems should arise regarding treatment issues.

Individual Providers

I believe there will always be a place for the individual provider, but the resources are becoming more limited. If you do not want to get involved with a group, either streamline your office to manage the paperwork and billing needed for MCOs, or hire someone to do it for you. Otherwise, you will spend many nonbillable hours performing these functions.

Another alternative to joining a group is simply to start a support group for individual practitioners working with managed care. As a group, you can problem-solve the issues that arise. Since you do not market your services as a group, there is no liability. You will need to keep clinical discussions at a minimum since this can open the door on liability in some regions. If you have any liability concerns, I recommend you consult with an attorney in your area.

Working as an individual, you don't have to adhere to a group's practice standards or treatment protocols, but you should think about these for yourself. If you want to understand what the practice standards are for your profession, contact your professional association and ask for a copy. Treatment protocols are published by the American Psychiatric Press, Inc. for many diagnoses.

There are those who say there is no good managed care company; I believe generalizations are risky. My experience has been that there are some MCOs I do not want to work with for many reasons—administrative, clinical, or a combination. Some companies are difficult to reach and coordinate information, slow to pay, or excessive in their paperwork demands. Others are well organized in their administrative functions but reluctant to allow treatment even when it is deemed necessary and still within the benefits package. And there are companies that offer good administrative functions along with a willingness to authorize treatment options when clinically indicated and contained in the benefits package. If you work with MCO clients, you will have increased paperwork, limitations on your clinical choices, reduced fees, and required practice standards or recommended approaches to diagnosis or treatment planning. If you find any of these unacceptable, you can focus on developing other avenues for your business while keeping an eye on how managed care evolves. You can do this by subscribing to one or more of the following journals (I have included phone numbers):

- *Psychotherapy Finances* (1-800-869-8450).
- *Behavioral Healthcare Tomorrow* (1-415-435-9821).
- *Strategies and Solutions* (1-800-497-0403).
- *Open Minds* (1-717-334-1329).
- *Practice Management Monthly* (1-800-578-5013).
- *Managed Care Strategies* (1-800-869-8450).

You can also find information on the Internet. Here are a few sites to get you started:

- YAHOO at http://www.yahoo.com.
- Interpsych is a newsletter you can subscribe to online. Send e-mail to: listserv@fra.psych.nemc.org; in the body of the e-mail, type "subscribe ipn."
- Stanford University at http://matia.stanford.edu/cogsci/org.html.
- University of California Santa Cruz at http://mambo.ucsc.edu/psl/psych.html.
- Psychology at http://www.princeton.edu/~harnad/psyc.html.
- Dr. Bob's Mental Health Links at http://uhs.bsd.uchicago.edu/~bhsiung/mental.html.
- Mental Health Home Page at http://www.mentalhealth.com.

Niche Marketing

This term is used in the managed care and marketing arenas to describe the promotion of a specialty in an area in which providers are seeking services. The trap for clinicians who develop specialties is that they tend to follow the needs of the provider groups rather than their own motivated skills. *Psychotherapy Finances* published a bonus edition in 1996, which was a report on the top niche specialty areas. The best approach is to define your own specialty areas, refer to the needs coming from the MCOs, and look for some kind of match.

Group Providers

Some managed care companies prefer to work with groups because it reduces their efforts to find an appropriate treatment specialist. There does not seem to be a preferred form of the group or legal type of entity, but a recent California study found that the most successful group practices, over time, were professional corporations. Any group must form some kind of legal entity or it cannot sign a contract. Checks are issued to the group, not to individuals. If the members of the group want to protect themselves from the wrongdoing of any associate, they need to discuss this matter with the holder of their malpractice insurance policy. They may need to carry individual practice policies as well as the one for the group. Often groups create indemnification agreements that limit individual liability for others' behavior, but it is not clear that they would protect them in any legal action. Anyway, it is always best to seek the advice of an attorney in your region who knows the laws you are dealing with and can guide you wisely.

There are many different ways to form groups. Here are some examples:

- *Preferred Provider Organization (PPO).* This is an organization of independent providers who have joined together to offer discounted, fee-for-services through a managed care contract. The PPO arranges for services to be provided but does not provide the services.

- *Independent Practice Association (IPA).* The providers practice independently and partially integrate their practices by sharing risk in managed care contracting. Usually it is a professional corporation or partnership owned by the participating providers.
- *Group without Walls (GWW).* In this configuration, individual practitioners remain in their own offices but centralize referral and billing services. They may operate under a DBA (Doing Business As) but do not share liability for a central site. They share economic risk for treatment services.
- *On-Site Traditional Group Practice.* These professionals all operate out of one or more sites and share site costs. The benefits are the ability to offer multispecialty, multidiscipline, one-stop shopping with quick decision making to respond to the changing marketplace. The legal structure is often a partnership, a professional corporation, or a limited liability professional corporation.
- *Management Service Organization (MSO).* This organization offers management services to professionals such as contracting, billing, computerization, group purchasing services, and outcome measures, and other management activities on request.
- *Alternative Service or Carve-Out Services.* A group of professionals can come together to offer specialized services to a managed care company. Services can include alcohol prevention and treatment, stress prevention and treatment, work and family problems, psychoeducation, and other prevention services.

Starting a Group

Many behavioral healthcare consultants work with providers to create group practices. *Psychotherapy Finances* periodically lists consultants across the nation. The following basic steps are essential for any newly formed group:

- Develop a mission statement that includes the group purpose and what services it will provide.
- Define your group structure and the legal entity that match the purposes in the mission statement.
- Begin your business plan including an attorney and accountant as part of the process.
- Select the group's clinical protocols and practice guidelines. These will provide your customers with information on the ways in which the group will provide consistent services.
- Create a quality assurance program that includes outcomes measures. The outcomes measures should be an extension of the practice guidelines and clinical protocols.
- Start your marketing plan. Include marketing to private-pay, managed care, public sector, and employer customers.

Successful groups include:

- A single point of access for clients.
- A single billing function.
- A toll-free phone number.
- Immediate access to treatment.
- On-call capacity.
- Crisis intervention resources.

- Connections to inpatient and alternative treatment sources.
- Multidisciplinary staff including psychiatrists.
- Ability to meet the needs of their geographic population.
- Use of sophisticated legal and financial advice.
- Shared fiscal risk.
- Ownership by either stockholders or partners.
- Electronic billing.
- Problem-focused treatment protocols.
- Ongoing treatment review, case management, and the ability to manage difficult cases.
- Outcomes measures.
- Continuous Quality Improvement (CQI) program.

It has been my experience in working with groups that the preceding items are key to becoming a successful group practice. Many groups come together with great ideas but cannot agree on how to structure their group. I have seen groups proceed without this structure but never reach fiscal success or develop long-run stability. The easiest step is the mission statement and services to be offered. Once these are in place, a consultation with an attorney and financial consultant helps members understand the new business arena they are entering. Creating a business plan will separate the workers from the nonworkers. There are usually some who want to attain group status effortlessly and those who are willing to do the hard work needed to put it in place. If this separation begins, the group needs to decide how to share the workload so the few who are doing the tasks do not burn out or grow resentful. Finally, when it comes to practice standards and treatment protocols, individual preferences need to be considered and a standardized approach agreed on. This can be a difficult time requiring honest communication and consideration of each professional's needs. It is usually easier for a small core group to develop the practice's structure and later bring on other members. In any case, setting up a group structure can be exciting and frustrating. It always requires motivation and perseverance.

HOW TO ASSESS A MANAGED CARE SYSTEM

There is a national group called the American Managed Behavioral Healthcare Association (AMBHA) that sets standards for managed behavioral health care delivery. So far their criteria for performance seem to reflect the needs of the private sector rather than the public sector. The standards also seem to address procedural efficiency, rather than the treatment outcomes. There is a great need for consumer advocacy groups to vocalize their issues and help create the measures needed to ensure quality care. The areas to measure are:

- *Access to Care.* What individuals are served, what alternatives there are to inpatient care, and how persistent mental illness is managed.
- *Consumer Satisfaction.* What is the level of patient satisfaction? What is the time interval to the patient's first appointment?
- *Quality of Care.* Describe the continuity of care, availability of medication for schizo-

phrenia, and treatment failure for substance abuse.

Patient Confidentiality Policies and Safeguards

When you have gotten past the stage of "just let me on the panel" to "what panel do I want to be on," consider the following about the MCO you are thinking about doing business with:

- *How Long the Company Has Been in the Marketplace.* MCOs come and go. You don't want to be a part of one that goes quickly.
- *Ease of Working with the Company.* You won't really know this until you have worked with the organization for a while. But you can ask colleagues who have worked with this MCO about their experiences.
- *Timeliness of Payment.* There is a national mandate that MCOs pay their providers within 30 days of billing. Some do not follow this mandate and find ways to extend the time by asking for more paperwork. Again, ask your colleagues.
- *Directory of Providers.* It is to your advantage for the consumer to use a directory to locate a provider. With that arrangement, you are not affected by provider ratings or referral references at the home office.
- *The Number and Types of Referrals in Your Region.* This will indicate whether there is a good match between your services and their needs.
- *Qualifications of Utilization Reviewers.* Who is authorizing treatment? Are the reviewers qualified professionals or general office workers?
- *Appeal Procedures.* If you have a problem regarding treatment authorization, what recourse do you have?
- *Quality Assurance Practices.* Is the company keeping an eye on itself and improving its services?

Working with Managed Care Companies—What They Want and What You'll Need

Whether the mental health practitioner chooses to work as an independent agent or join others to form a group, there are some things each person needs to have in place to work in the managed care arena. If you are considering such a venture, you will need the following essentials:

General Needs

- A license or certification.
- A resume.
- Specialties and the training received to support any specialty.
- Educational transcripts.
- Professional and clinical experience.
- A clinical orientation that is compatible with MCO short-term strategic approach.
- Malpractice coverage.
- A clear practice record.
- Coverage for your practice when you are not available.
- A practice management tool or system that tracks payment and holds client treatment records. Your client treatment records need to be problem oriented and behaviorally measured.

- A team of experts for use when needed:

  Primary care physician for physicals.
  Psychiatrist for psychopharmacological consultation.
  Nutritionist (especially important for eating disorder specialties).
  Psychologist for testing.
  Attorney for legal and liability issues.
  CPA for fiscal management and planning.

Office Systems You Need

- *Office.* The office itself needs to be comfortable and clean. It should have adequate parking, lighting, and access to public transportation, and should be wheelchair accessible.
- *Communication.* You need a telephone in the office, an answering system or service, and a fax machine. You might also consider a beeper to help you pick up telephone messages immediately.
- *Computerization.* A computer helps you manage your client records and billing. It also allows you to bill electronically. It is likely that all MCOs will move to electronic billing in the future.

Basic Forms and Practice Policies

- *Financial Policy.* This includes what your fees are, how you would like to be paid, how you handle insurance, and what you do about delinquent accounts.
- *New Client Information.* New clients should receive printed information about confidentiality, how to reach you outside their appointments, the consequences of psychotherapy, alternatives to psychotherapy, and any other information you feel is important for them.
- *Consent for Treatment.* This is a printed form providing consent to treat the adults or children you are seeing.
- *Release of Information.* You need one of these forms for any outside contact you make regarding your client. This includes insurance billing and medical reports.
- *Assignment of Benefits.* This gives you the authority to accept insurance payment directly rather than passing it through the client.
- *Outcome Measures.* This will provide you with the information you need for a practice assessment and helps you understand your practice patterns. You need to include client satisfaction, symptom relief, and general functionality.
- *A Practice Assessment.* Your practice assessment should include:

  The types of clients you see by age and *DSM* diagnosis.

  The communities your clients live in, usually collected by zip codes.

  The average number of sessions you provide per client or diagnosis.

  The average duration of treatment for the same.

  Your average fee and average total cost of treatment.

  Your current payor mix, (e.g., MCO, direct pay).

  The average number of sessions you provide per month.

  The average wait between the first contact and the first appointment.

The number of psychiatric hospitalizations you have required.

- *Abandonment Policy.* What will you do when a client's benefits are exhausted and the client still needs treatment?

Skills You Need

- *Case Management.* You are part of a treatment system when you work with managed care. You are not only managing your treatment plan, you are also managing resources. You must work within your clients' insurance benefits, know who to refer to when they step outside your scope of expertise, and access the resources in the community that can support clients when they leave treatment.
- *Treatment Planning and Outpatient Treatment Reports (OTR).* The utilization reviewer is the person who authorizes medically necessary treatment. Any treatment that is primarily for "personal growth" is not medically necessary. The best way to ensure approval for treatment requests is to have a solid treatment plan based on the *DSM* that includes your diagnosis, short- and long-term treatment goals, and planned interventions. The plan needs to show how you will help the client reach the treatment goals. Projected change needs to be observable and measurable.
- *Diagnostic Skills.* You must know how to use the *DSM.* There are several books that train you and courses that help you use this system. If you choose to work with managed care, this is essential. The diagnosis should include a detailed symptom description. For example, if you are working with an eating disorder and your client is purging, include when and how often the person is purging. Include a full five-axes diagnosis. Also include any "Rule Out" diagnosis and the information you need to gather to make your decision. Include how the client is functioning in all areas of life, family, work, and other relationships. Include the severity of stressors and how they are affecting the client.
- *Treatment Approaches.* If you use a treatment approach that isn't widely accepted such as a systems approach or hypnosis, explain your rationale.
- *The Treatment Team and Support Systems.* Be sure to include the other members of the treatment team such as the primary care physician, prescribing psychiatrist, nutritionist, or other professional involved in the client's treatment. Also include any community resources your client can benefit from.
- *Requests for Further Treatment.* When you request further visits instead of "weekly psychotherapy" you can state weekly cognitive therapy with behavioral rehearsal. Use whatever approaches you are expert in but elaborate on what will be done. If you cannot estimate how many visits you need, ask for visits for three to six months with a commitment to be more explicit at the next update.
- *Informed Consent.* The client needs to be fully informed about the details of the treatment plan.

Many of these tools can be found in two sets of practice management publications:

- *The Paper Office* (Zuckerman & Guyett, 1991).
- *The Foundations of Your Private Practice* (Gold, 1994).

Finding the MCOs You Want to Work With

An MCO that wants to provide services in your state must register with them. You can get this information on request from your state insurance commissioner. There are also companies that sell names of MCOs. Contact your national professional association for a list of resources or look in the advertising section of professional publications. A resource I have used is Professional Health Plan (tel. 1-510-601-8033). I find the best way is to subscribe to one of the managed care periodicals and watch for announcements of open panels. Several publications mentioned earlier are also helpful here. They include *Psychotherapy Finances, Open Minds, Practice Management Monthly,* and *Managed Care Strategies.*

Getting on Panels

Call or write the MCO you want to work with and ask about its open enrollment dates. If the company is accepting providers, get the name of the person or department receiving requests and send a *request for proposal to become a panel provider.* If you don't have a name or department, address your cover letter to *Provider Relations.* Include:

- Why you want to be on this MCO panel.
- Location of your office and accessibility (parking, public transportation, wheelchair accessible).
- University you graduated from and any special training you have received.
- Your licenses and specialties.
- Number of years in practice.
- Your commitment to short-term strategic treatment. If you have done any outcome studies on your clients, you can include a practice summary with your letter.
- If you do any of your own testing, describe what kind.
- If you have a practice newsletter, send a copy with your letter.
- List other MCOs you already work with. Do not name more than three.
- State second languages spoken.
- Explain how you assure quality. This could be an outcomes measurement system or a quality management process.

With your cover letter include:

- Vitae or resume.
- Continuing education class verifications and training you have implemented.
- Your practice brochure.
- Copies of your license(s) and certifications.
- A copy of your malpractice insurance cover sheet.

Note your responses, fill out and return the applications you receive, and track your developing relationships with these MCOs. Any nonresponder can be approached again after you do a little research about the company and its specific needs.

More Ideas to Get on Panels

- Fill a geographic need in the MCO's delivery system. You can set up a satellite office by subletting from a colleague.

- Ask about the MCO's training needs and offer free training to its staff in an area in which you have expertise.
- Offer to treat an underserved population.
- Offer short-term groups.
- Offer services for young children.
- Don't offer services that are outside Axis I *DSM* diagnoses; they are seldom covered.
- Take a case manager to lunch.

Maintaining a High Provider Profile

Managed care organizations have started a provider profile system: "A" providers get a large majority of referrals; "B" providers get some referrals; and "C" providers get no referrals. The profile criteria measure the following six areas:

1. Utilization or cost per client case.
2. Clinical outcomes; how well treatment goals were met.
3. Process performance or the quality of communication between the case manager and the provider.
4. Technical performance such as the use of targeted focal therapy.
5. Patient satisfaction with the provider's environment or office.
6. Patient satisfaction with the therapist.

Client surveys provide information for items 2, 5, and 6; case manager evaluations provide information for items 3 and 4. Item 1 is measured by the utilization or average number of sessions per patient. The goal is to identify the most cost-effective and efficient providers.

Ways to Enhance Your Profile

- Be sensitive to the care manager's needs.
- Maintain a friendly relationship rather than an adversarial one.
- Be accessible and quickly responsive.
- Submit billing and reports in a timely manner.
- Consider yourself as part of a team.
- Make treatment plans concrete and specific to the problem you are addressing. Include short-term goals, long-term goals, and treatment interventions. Be clear about how you will help your client reach the treatment goals you have identified.
- Notify the care manager when new problems emerge or treatment is not going as you have planned.

Filling Out the Contracts

Don't just sign a new contract no matter how excited you are about getting on a panel. Read it carefully and ask yourself whether you can live with this agreement. Many consultants suggest changing the contract to meet your needs. If you cannot accept the contract as is, call the company and speak with someone who understands the contract and has some decision-making ability. Just making changes to your contract may not matter at all. Many new contracts carry a statement at the end that essentially says any changes made to the contract are not recognized. Things to look out for are:

- Who carries the liability if the MCO makes a mistake? It should not be you.
- What kind of access does the MCO have to your records? Some companies require

complete access to all client records. This may not be acceptable to you.

- Some have gag rules. This means you cannot tell your client about alternative forms of treatment even if they are called for.
- The best option is to have an attorney review the contract, translate it into understandable terms, and advise you of your responsibilities if you sign.

Outcome Measures

The assessment of clinical outcomes and patient satisfaction has become a key component of managed care. Outcome measures are believed to maintain quality and provide information on the best treatment for specific problems. There appears to be some agreement that outcomes should assess three areas:

- The level of psychiatric symptoms.
- Clinical functioning.
- Patient satisfaction.

Short-term measures are best focused on symptom assessment and long-term measures on the functional assessment.

The following outcome measurement tools are in the public domain. That means they can be copied and used without charge. You may want to pay a one-time fee for a good printed copy and the training materials to use the instrument:

Severity of Symptoms

The BASIS-32 is widely used. The client fills it out at intake, discharge, and then several months after treatment. Contact Sue Eisen at McLean Hospital, 115 Mill St., Belmont MA 02178-9106, 617-855-2425. They have a packet of information available for $50.

Substance Abuse

The Addiction Severity Index (ASI) assesses substance abuse problems. Contact Delta-Metrics, One Commerce Square, Ste. 1020, Philadelphia, PA 19103, 800-238-2433 for a price list, cost $1.

Functionality

The Global Assessment of Function (GAF) is included in the *DSM-IV* manual (APA, 1994). It can be self-administered or used by the clinician. A GAF assessment can be used at the beginning, periodicaly during treatment, at discharge, and weeks after the client has terminated.

Client Satisfaction

This measure does not need to correlate with the other measures. Clients may be happy with their treatment even if the outcomes are poor. The outcomes may be positive and the client satisfaction low. Client satisfaction often includes functions such as promptness, friendliness, cleanliness of the office, easy access, and simplicity in billing procedures.This questionnaire is filled out by the client at the conclusion of treatment and again three to six months later. It is fairly easy for practitioners to create their own client satisfaction surveys, or they can use the following one: Client Satisfaction Questionnaire available from the Association for Ambulatory Behavioral Healthcare (AABH) 301 N. Fairfax St., Ste. 109, Alexandria, VA 22314-2696, 703-836-2274.

Staying Viable

Stress the quality of your services. Quality is measured through outcome studies. Gather information and report favorable outcomes:

- Take training in brief therapy, substance abuse, and any other area you declare as a specialty.
- Develop programs or treatments for specific diagnosis or focal problems.
- Regularly contact EAPs and MCOs to find out what specialties or services they are looking for.
- Call the MCOs you either have a relationship with or want to develop a relationship with and find out the name of the person who makes referrals to your area. Compile a mailing list and mail them newsletters and other marketing pieces.
- Invite local MCOs to seminars, open houses, or workshops.
- Identify the area companies with which the MCO has contracts. Call these companies and get a list of their key personnel, benefits specialists, and EAP staff. Add these individuals to your mailing list. Offer these companies training workshops. Get the practice guidelines from the MCOs you are contracted with and follow them.

Brief Therapy Models

MCOs emphasize brief treatment. With the growth of managed care, there has been a flood of brief treatment models in the marketplace. These models have some commonalities.

Focus on What the Client Wants from You

This may be a different approach from the ones you were trained in. You need to hold clients accountable as primary change agents and increase their awareness of their own resources. Ask what they want as an outcome to therapy and how they would measure success.

Focus on Client Strengths and Positives

This will change the session from a problem-focused event to a solution-focused event. This gives clients a sense of control and participation in their treatment. Solicit your clients' ideas for solutions to their problems.

Build Client Introspection

You can use hypothetical questions to get clients to think about their problems as evaluators rather than as reactors. The questions also give you information about how clients view their internal world and resources. Their responses clarify whether the problem is internal or external. Ideally, the questions allow clients to think as a third person observing their own process in solving problems.

Focus on Change

Focus clients' attention on change and how it happens. Change can be broken down into small steps so clients can always be successful. This approach also helps clients consider new choices in making new decisions. Support any kind of action toward creating change.

Create Treatment Contracts

You can work with clients to make contracts identifying short- and long-term treatment goals. This helps clients see the positive change that takes place instead of getting lost in their current problems. The long-term contract with self will also help clients after they leave the therapy environment.

Use Homework to Keep Clients on Track

Assign tasks between sessions to empower clients outside the individual session. Ask clients what they believe is under their control and what they need help to change. After assessing their abilities, provide them with new skills and tools to create the change they seek. After they have done their homework, ask them to evaluate how things are going. Encourage them to voice their perceptions of how effective they are being at creating personal change. Support their own creativity in helping themselves create the changes they seek.

All of these steps support the change process (Prochaska & DiClemente, 1982):

- Precontemplation of the change.
- Contemplation of the change.
- Decision making about the change.
- Action.
- Maintenance of the new state.

The following brief treatment model provides structure for a 10-session plan:

Session 1: Assessment and alliance building.

Session 2. Solidify alliance around contractual agreement.

Sessions 3–6. Psychoeducation, skill building, reassessment of goals.

Sessions 7–9. Skill implementation, successive enhancement of adjustment tool kit.

Session 10. Termination, maintenance, and relapse prevention.

MANAGED CARE DONE WELL

In the ideal system, everybody is covered and there is a systemwide creativity in problem solving. The public and the family assume responsibility for what they can provide and have input into the larger systems. Professionals study the needs of the culture, and delivery of services is based on the needs identified in the field of study. Care is based on short-term need and long-term solutions. Business makes a profit and also supports the larger economy. The mental health profession is viewed as a whole and delivers services based on individual professional strengths.

TRANSITIONING OUT OF MANAGED CARE

Stepping Out of the Managed Care Trance

Many professionals believe they will not survive unless they continue to work with MCOs. There is simply too much diversity in this country to have to rely on any single system for your livelihood. I find that whether a professional can work outside an MCO structure depends on how willing the person is to commit to marketing in other arenas. Many professionals have chosen to not accept managed care and are succeeding, even flourishing. Others have not gotten involved with managed care, have not marketed their services in other ways, and find their practices growing smaller and smaller.

In some ways, we have been brainwashed by the media to believe the individual practitioner is a dying breed; if you are not part of managed care, you may as well consider another profession. Remember, we each have our own reality and yours can be free of managed care.

The trick becomes shifting your referral base away from managed care organizations while you are developing other referral bases. I do not suggest anyone call up the MCOs they work for and say *no more* before developing other client sources. There are many directions to move in. You can market yourself to:

- The private pay marketplace.
- The "unhappy with managed care" population.
- The "I don't want my mental health records in anyone's computer" group.
- Employee assistance programs.
- Private industry.
- Schools.
- Agencies.

One way of convincing yourself to make the change is to track the time you invest in paperwork, telephone calls, and therapy sessions. Divide that time into the fees you have received and see what your hourly figure is. You may be surprised. There is a start-up time cost for developing new markets but often the long-term payoff more than balances that investment.

9

CHANGE, INNOVATION, AND MAINTENANCE OF SUCCESS

The pursuit of success, in accordance with your own desires, is a truly compelling path. Too many people believe that success is a singular event, a great race that was won, or one goal achieved. Defining success in this way makes it finite. Consciously creating your future is an evolutionary process of continually learning from your experiences and then applying a new understanding and ability to shape and create increasingly superior results. Success then becomes a process rather than a goal.

Change is a constant. A constant-change process model has a style and strategy. You will find that you change in one arena for a time and then reach a point where the arena itself must change. I call this "inner change" and "outer change." You choose, plan, manage, honor your creativity and intuition, and listen to your heart. As you change internally and change takes place externally, the two dialogue with one another until it is time for a major paradigm shift to something that may not have existed before. The paradigm shift calls for *breakthrough,* innovation, or out-of-the-box thinking. You need to relax, let go of old beliefs, mourn your losses, and allow your inner knowing and innate creativity and power to take charge and shape the future. This change and innovation process cannot take place when you are bound up with stress or living out of balance. This chapter offers tools and ideas to maintain your own wellness. Your personal power sets the stage for change, creativity, and innovation.

Succeeding through Change

A Changing Profession

You probably have some ideas about what you believe you need to know to ensure future success. The good news is you need to have a positive view; the bad news is you will never have all the information. The task becomes living with positive uncertainty.

Information becomes obsolete quickly and there is too much to process. All information is colored by the sender and receiver; there is no virgin information. In your mind's eye, you are imagining the past and the future and forming the information into paradigms to support your beliefs. Think of your life as something you are watching from a deck chair on a cruise ship. Some people look at the wake of the ship and focus on the past. Others sit up in the bow with an eye only to the future. People in the best position keep an eye on both.

Professional Competence and Change

Competence in a profession can be the enemy of consciousness and change. The profession begins not to recognize its incompetence. Reflect on Freud and the personal boundaries he violated with his early clients by maintaining close relationships with them and their families. As the profession proceeded, clinicians began to identify the behaviors and methodologies that supported competence and advocated for practice guidelines. Defining how the profession should operate, however, caused practitioners to lose sight of the changing environment, and unconsciously they again became incompetent in relation to the new social paradigm and its needs. *The key to professional competence is to maintain a constant dialogue between the expertise of the profession and the new needs of the environment.* The behavioral healthcare industry has addressed some of those needs by championing short-term, symptom-specific treatment. Many individuals did not want to spend years in psychodynamic therapy; they just wanted to help their children or deal with a divorce.

Dynamics of Professional Change

To identify change, you first need to know its current state. The mental health profession must be clarified internally and then in relation to its environment. Most professionals don't take the time to look at the entire profession and how it has helped create the problems they face today. When you look inside the mental health profession, think about it in terms of:

- Who's in and who's out?
- What are the boundaries between the mental health profession and other professions?
- What kind of communication goes on within the profession?
- Who is responsible for this communication and how consistent is it?
- Is there a formal authority system and does it reflect your values?
- What is the informal authority system?
- What are the rewards of the profession?
- How are conflicts resolved?
- Who are the heroes?
- Who are the decision makers about your profession?
- What kinds of leadership styles are there?
- What are the profession's goals?

Now, looking at outside influences, ask yourself:

- What's the direct and indirect competition to mental health services?
- What new technologies and methodologies create change in the field? Do international players pose a threat or additional opportunities?
- Who are the key players in the industry and where are they now?
- What new regional, state, or federal regulations affect the profession?
- What consumer issues affect the industry?

- Who is initiating major advances?
- What are the sociological and demographic factors?
- How do trends such as the aging of Americans impact the industry?
- What are people spending money on in the field?

It is important to do this kind of analysis for any professional area you are working in or considering entering. If you want to enter the consulting, motivational speaking, or training industry, answer these questions from that perspective.

Now evaluate yourself in relation to your current field, and then for any you are considering entering. Examine how you want to reposition yourself and assess whether you are willing and able to meet the challenges of change:

- What are your transferable skills?

  Communication.
  Negotiating skills.
  Supervision.
  Other.
- Is the culture of the industry in tune with you?
- How transferable are your values?
- How adaptable are you?
- Do you need to reeducate yourself?

  What new skills do you need?

  What schools are most respected in these fields?
  List four.
- Publications:

  What are the most important industry trade publications?
  List four.
- What is the dress code? Would you fit in or do you need to remake your personal presentation?
- How would you demonstrate seriousness and commitment to your current or new field?
- What associations can you join?
- What boards can you serve on?
- What committees can you volunteer for?
- What certificates, licenses, and degrees matter? Are you willing to do what it takes to get these credentials?

How Do You View the Future?

It is helpful to understand how you view the future. Here are some metaphors:

- *Roller Coaster.* Fixed and determined with lots of bumpy change.
- *Rushing River.* Rushing forward in a fixed direction needing navigation around the obstacles.
- *Vast Ocean.* Calm and violent needing a wise navigator to choose directions.
- *Crap Shoot.* Entirely random, with a goal of just playing the game.
- *Mystery Play.* Constantly watching your back and looking for clues to understand an event.
- *An Experiment.* Looking for what works, constantly putting new ideas together to see what happens.

Create your own metaphor of your beliefs about the future. The most important point is that you have a model for the future and a belief that it can unfold in your best interests. Having a vision of the future helps you predict and prepare for change, imagine new ideas, and participate in their creation. Make your life a process not a destination.

Managing Change

Change comes to us in many ways:

- *Deliberate Change.* These changes are created intentionally. This could be the decision to move to a warmer climate.
- *Involuntary Change.* This can be in the form of an accident or some change that is imposed on you by another person or the environment.
- *Short-Term Change.* Your mother may come to stay with you for a week or you may have an unexpected expense that requires that you become more frugal for a time.
- *Long-Term or Progressive Change.* Aging is progressive change. It happens every day over a long period.

How Do You Know When It Is Time to Change?

Sometimes your mind and spirit may not send concrete enough information to validate that it is time for a professional change. Compassion fatigue is a common stress-related ailment of professional psychotherapists. Often we are so busy keeping our business and our clients afloat we lose sight of our own well-being. When you find yourself overextended in any arena you may need to step back and assess where you stand. A concrete approach is to check out how your body is doing. When the body is stressed, it is at a constant state of alert. It tells the brain to send messages that release hormones such as adrenaline and cortisol. These hormones trigger a series of instinctive physiological reactions known as the *fight-or-flight* response. The muscles contract, metabolism speeds up, breathing increases, the digestive system shuts down, and the blood flow to the arms and legs constricts so that too much blood isn't lost if there is an injury. These activities help prepare you for an encounter with an unfriendly bear. In today's workplace, these reactions can go on day after day. Research done by cardiologist Dean Ornish, explained in his book *Dr. Dean Ornish's Program for Reversing Heart Disease* (Ornish, 1990), shows that chronic stress causes a buildup of cholesterol and a narrowing of the arteries causing increased cardiovascular disease. Chronic stress also lowers the immune system leaving you at the mercy of the environment. Tension impairs the digestion of food opening the door on ulcers and other digestive problems. If you believe you are suffering from stress-related problems, ask yourself whether you have the following symptoms:

- Physical health—

  Insomnia.
  Headaches.
  High blood pressure.
  Sore jaw.
  Digestive problems.
  Menstrual irregularities.
  Muscle stiffness.
  Exhaustion upon waking.
  Irritability.

- Behavioral—

  Free-floating anxiety.
  Poor appetite or overeating.
  Withdrawal from social activities.
  Lack of interest in sex.
  Forgetfulness.

Preoccupation with what you need to do next.
Difficulty having fun.
Lessened sense of humor.
Overwhelmed by too much to do with too little time.
Increase in the use of alcohol, caffeine, or drugs (prescription or street).

What Can You Do to Create Healthy Change?

Change unfolds in a series of six change-stages. You can identify what stage you are in at any time (Prochaska, Norcross, & DiClemente, 1994):

1. Precontemplation.
2. Contemplation.
3. Preparation.
4. Action.
5. Maintenance.
6. Termination.

Change is generally not linear. Relapse or a return to an earlier stage is the norm rather than the exception. Relapse is not a sign of weakness: It is a sign of normality. It is simply telling you there is more work for you to do in the stage you have returned to. When you are stabilized in that area, you will move on. A good model to use is a spiral. Each time you return to a stage, you are entering from a higher level than when you started. The spiral may continue but it is reaching higher levels of development at each turn.

Precontemplation

This stage is earmarked with denial. "People at this stage usually have no intention of changing their behavior, and typically deny having a problem" (Prochaska et al., 1994). Precontemplators want to change everyone else who is bothering them rather than change themselves. An example is the private practitioner whose income has decreased significantly, blames managed care for the loss, and believes if they just wait long enough things will turn themselves around. They avoid learning anything about their problem even though their behavior may be self-defeating or damaging. It is the self-damaging behavior that often is the trigger that moves them to the next stage.

Contemplation

"In the contemplation state, people acknowledge that they have a problem and begin to think seriously about solving it" (Prochaska et al., 1994). People at the stage of contemplation are not ready to change yet but they are willing to be aware of the problem and possible solutions.

Preparation

The planning of change begins in this stage. Ambivalence is a key word for this stage. There may have already been small attempts toward change such as subscribing to professional publications, and the individual's awareness is high regarding the problem. It is not a good idea at this stage to leap into a solution. You need to use this time for careful planning and understanding of the complete change process including maintenance and termination.

Action

Action requires commitment of time and resources. This stage has the greatest visibility and vulnerability. A great deal of change has already taken place, but it has been more internal than external and not as noticeable. After the action toward change begins, there is a lot of reinforcement. As the changed behavior continues, support dwindles and the individual is left to his or her own reinforcing behaviors. When relapse is visible to others, the person often feels like a failure. He or she needs to understand that relapse is simply part of the process and mark the point at which it occurred. The overall progress will be apparent when the person returns to action.

Maintenance

Change does not end with the action stage. The change must be stabilized in maintenance. This stage can last from six months to a lifetime. The subtle benefits of the action stage are seen during this time. The maintenance stage requires both internal and external reinforcing events.

Termination

The termination stage is simply the platform for another change process to begin. The former problem or behavior is no longer a temptation and there is no fear of its return. The person will remember the previous problem but usually will not be enticed to "go there" again. The struggle is over for most although some will always carry traces of temptation with them.

The key to successful change is knowing where you stand and understanding the best use of coping skills for that stage.

Identifying Your Stage of Change

It is easy to identify the change-stage you are in. Before you can focus on that stage, you must identify what the problem is. Sometimes others do not see a problem and you do. This is time for a reality check. Some women with anorexia believe they are fat when they are quite thin. Decide whether you agree or disagree with the following statements (Prochaska et al., 1994), and answer yes or no accordingly:

1. I solved my problem more than six months ago.
2. I have taken action on my problem within the past six months.
3. I am intending to take action in the next month.
4. I am intending to take action in the next six months.

A resounding no to all these statements puts you in the precontemplation stage. Contemplators will have only answered no to Numbers 3 and 4. A pattern of yes to Numbers 3 and 4 and no to the others is the preparation stage. A no to Number 1 and yes to Number 2 is the action stage. When you have answered yes to all the questions you have reached maintenance. If you have identified your work as a problem area, it will help to know what stage of change you are in.

Change Strategies

If you believe it is time for a change, the first step is to take charge, identify the stress in your body, and do something about it. Start with relaxation exercises or yoga and enforced quiet time or meditation. Get realistic about how much time you have in your day and how much you can reasonably expect to accomplish. When you are done, let go and make plans about what you need to eliminate from your list of things to do. Take control of your eating, exercising, and sleeping habits. If you don't know what is right for you, consult with professionals. Ask yourself if you are doing the work you love. Perhaps all you need to do is look again at your work and see if there are ways to change it to meet your needs. If the answer is no, then you need a greater level of change.

Letting Go of the Old

It is important to stay aware of your feelings during the change process and to deal with emotions that arise as soon as possible. Stifling your feelings will lead to a stress reaction that will interfere with the smooth flow of change.

Change and Your Emotions

Whether you are letting go of a positive aspect in your life or a negative one, you will grieve its loss. If you are changing how you conceptualize your vocation you will experience a loss. Grieve the loss of the old and move toward the future.

There are several stages to the grief process. Most therapists are familiar with them but I am listing them below as a refresher. I have included those identified by Elizabeth Kubler-Ross (1993) as well as other stages I have observed in my clients. They include:

- *Denial.* A lack of awareness that a loss has taken place. This could be the professional whose income has decreased or paperwork increased, but they don't believe the changes are a threat.
- *Fear.* When the fiscal impact on the private practice has become a threat and the stress of increased time needed to manage casework has impacted lifestyle, the loss of time and money can trigger fears of even greater losses. Many practitioners fear taking themselves off panels and continue to spend time on paperwork when they could be focusing on marketing to private pay arenas. Talk about your fears with yourself, and ask yourself how you can come to terms with them. If you need to speak with another, seek out help.
- *Anger.* Although anger is a natural reaction to loss, you should be careful not to direct it destructively or inappropriately. Anger is often directed toward the BHOs. It is important to identify the source of the anger and ask yourself how you can express it creatively rather than destructively.
- *Guilt.* Many of us feel guilty after a loss, as if it is shameful to have lost something or let it go. Guilt usually serves no purpose except to increase your own stress. It can be a useless emotion unless you have indeed harmed another; then guilt may motivate you to make amends.
- *Bartering.* People often attempt to give away something else to get back what they lost or extrapolate the barter into the future so they will never have the same kind of loss again. The most important aspect is to ask yourself whether the exchange is appropriate. Will any kind of barter make a difference, or is it appropriate for the future?
- *Depression.* Depression can be frightening to some who have had previous experiences with this state. Unless there is an underlying clinical depression in addition to the natural grief response, it will pass just like the common cold. This is a good time to work in your journal and reflect on how the loss has changed your life. If the depression affects your life

significantly or lasts more than three months, seek professional help.

- *Relief.* Often people feel guilty about feeling relief after a loss. It is all right to feel relieved and ready to move in new directions.

Death and loss are a natural process and when something passes away, something new will always take its space. Stepping away from years of practicing in a particular way is courageous and you should prepare for some kind of grief reaction.

Maintaining a Solid Foundation in a Changing Environment

In today's society, people no longer reach adulthood and relax on their educational laurels. Your career will not proceed along a predetermined path. You may need to develop many professional careers during your working lifetime. That means you will have to be constantly learning and preparing for a new future. A solid foundation is one that is constantly reinforcing its pillars of knowledge. Take a wide range of continuing education courses. Include marketing, clinical, and other classes or seminars to keep in touch with the changing marketplace. When you choose a particular specialty, go to classes offered by others in your area to see what new approaches are developing. Network with others both within and outside your area of expertise. The wider and more diverse your foundation is, the better prepared you are for change and creativity.

Risk Taking

There is an old saying "You can't make anything without mistakes," which I have framed and is hanging on the wall in my office. Toddlers don't walk perfectly after taking their first step. They need to practice and try new ways of walking until they perfect this skill. The same holds true for life. If you are going to live a creative, dynamic life, you can look forward to making mistakes. Every mistake is an attempt to do something that has not yet been mastered. The mistake is exactly that—*a mis-take.* Now that you have had this experience, you can look for new ways of mastering the task. Risk taking involves trying new skills and behaviors so it is full of mis-takes.

There are different styles of risk taking. I like to use the image of a trapeze artist to describe the styles:

- *Developmental.* This performer prepares the setting and checks to make certain the safety net is in place. He or she climbs up the pole to the platform above the audience, grabs the trapeze, swings to the other side, grabs the new trapeze, lets go of the old one, and swings to safety. This risk taker develops plans well ahead and makes certain not to make changes before acquiring a replacement.
- *Transitional.* The second performer has faith in his or her preparation or the preparation of others. This artist climbs up to the platform, swings out, and leaps across to the new trapeze trusting it will be where it has always been in the past. This risk taker has some experience and carries a sense of trust about the transitions. He or she is confident that everything will be all right.
- *Transformational.* The performer is standing on the platform, which has just burst into flames. This artist must swing out and find something to save him or her because returning to the old platform is impossible.

What kind of risk taker are you in terms of changing your professional career?

Your Comfort Zone

When any large change is on the horizon, it threatens the safety of the known. You may need to change your personal value structure and internal definition of *self.* When you make these kinds of changes, you also affect the roles and relationships you play and have with others. Your comfort zone is threatened. Figure 9.1 is a visual representation of the change process involved in establishing a new comfort zone.

As you become more facile with change, you will find you can thrive on it. With this ease, you are better positioned to be an innovator in your profession since you no longer have to fear the consequences of change.

INNOVATION

Entrepreneurism versus Innovation

America fosters an entrepreneurial society. Being an entrepreneur is different from being an innovator. When you find a new way to make money on used tires, you are an innovator. An entrepreneur may start a business, but it may not be an innovation. If you open a drive-through used tire store, you are an entrepreneur. An entrepreneur shifts economic resources out of an area of lower productivity and into an area of greater yield (Drucker, 1985). McDonald's is a good example of entrepreneurial activity. The founder supplied hamburgers with a new model of fast food delivery. Nothing new was created, but the delivery was enhanced.

Mental health professionals are well trained to be successful innovators. Most have been trained to be aware of content in events as well as process. Innovation requires a sensitivity to both. An innovator endows resources with a new capacity to create profit. The mold that breeds penicillin was a pest in many researchers' laboratories until Alexander Fleming realized its potential as an effective bacterial killer. Systematic innovation is the search for changes that create economic or social innovation. Innovation exploits change. Peter Drucker, one of the early writers on innovation, has identified seven sources for innovative opportunity. The first four lie within the business and the next three are outside the business:

1. The unexpected success or failure.
2. Incongruity between a reality that is believed to exist and the reality as it is in the world.
3. Innovation founded in the processes of the business.
4. Change in the industry or field structure or the marketplace.
5. Population changes (demographics).
6. Changes in perception, mood, and meaning.
7. New knowledge or information or the convergence of known information or technology to create something new.

These sources can be applied to innovation in the field of mental health.

The Unexpected

The service or product with which you are achieving success is not the one you thought would fly. This symptom of the unexpected is a phenomenon that could reflect limited vision, knowledge, or understanding of a situation. In any case, rather than continue to push the

Figure 9.1

Establishing a New Comfort Zone

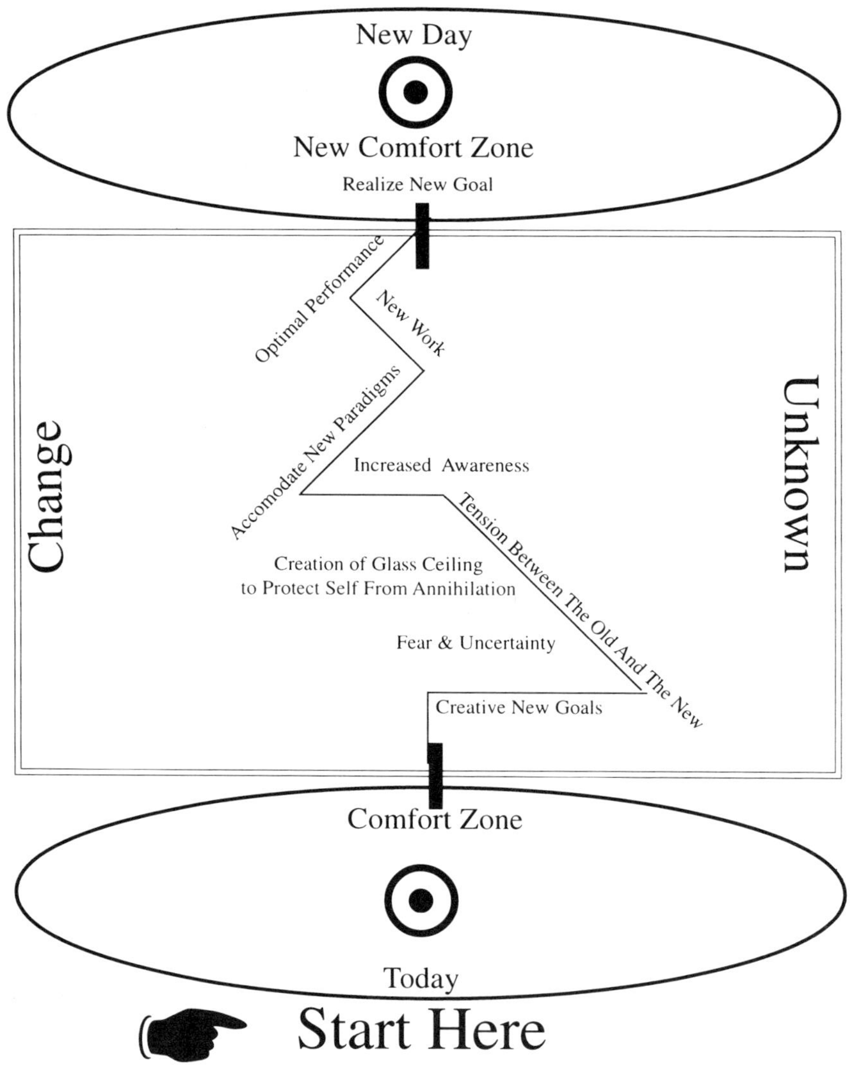

original product, the effective innovator needs to be ready to get behind the item the public has identified as the one they like.

An Incongruity

An incongruity is a dissonance between what is and what ought to be or between what is and what everybody assumes it to be. An incongruity is a symptom of an underlying fault or a change that has already happened or is about to happen. Incongruities are usually qualitative rather than quantitative and are visible to those within the field yet accepted as a norm not acted upon. Some current incongruities in the mental health field are:

- The differences between the perceived and actual client values and expectations and the goals of the clinician or agency.
- The disparity between the cost of mental healthcare and the resources of all levels of the population.
- The media's portrayal of therapists and their work and the reality of the profession.

All of these disparities need to be viewed as opportunities for innovation in the shaping and delivery of mental health services.

Process-Related Problems

A process need is task focused. The innovation perfects a process that already exists, replaces a weak link, or redesigns an existing process. There are process irregularities in many mental healthcare delivery systems. Clients in crisis may be placed on a waiting list for care. They may need family therapy but their therapist does not know of a referral resource that can fill their needs. Often a process need requires new information or techniques. Individual creativity is required for its innovation.

Change in the Industry or the Marketplace. The mental health field has seen tremendous changes in its industry in the past 15 years. Most of the change has been driven by the business industry and not by the professionals. Professionals are just beginning to meet the challenges by forming their own business entities to compete in the marketplace. The kind of field change we are currently experiencing is ripe with opportunity for innovation. One advantage the small professional practice has over the large MCO is its ability to make fast decisions and act quickly. This is an important lead. Once managed care has solidified their marketplace with the insured population, they will begin a frontal attack on the private marketplace. They will have millions of dollars to spend on marketing vehicles to convince people to use their services and products. You can get there first and begin to build client loyalty to compete with their marketing dollars.

Population Changes

America is getting older, teens are getting more chaotic, and families are in trouble. These changes provide opportunities for innovation in the creation and delivery of services. When you develop a new treatment approach or model that addresses these changes, you are positioning yourself for future success.

Changes in Perception, Mood, and Meaning

When a change in perception happens, the service or product may remain the same, but its meaning changes. With the call for equal benefits for mental and physical health, mental health is put on a new parity. Mental health now becomes just as important as physical health. Some of the stigma attached to mental illness may begin to dissipate. This creates a change in the perception of mental wellness by business and the population in general. The door opens for innovation in the positioning and delivery of mental health services.

New Knowledge or Information

We constantly hear of new ways of seeing what goes on in the brain. New treatment modalities emerge from the field. The Internet expands our access to information. All these and more impact the way mental health services can be used and offered. There are practitioners offering services on the Internet, and this means of communication is growing in quantum leaps daily. The field of mental health is often cautious about incorporating new knowledge or information into the mainstream profession, but I believe it can be ethically used as an opportunity for innovation.

Being Innovative

There are things you can do to be innovative in your field. Begin by looking at the preceding seven areas and identify opportunities that draw on your professional resources. Once you have some ideas to work with, start talking to others and asking questions. Keep asking yourself how your idea benefits your target population. Get their opinions. Don't try to do too many things with one innovation. Something new is often slow to take hold in the marketplace, and if your changes are too complex, you will lose your audience. Finally, don't innovate for future, innovate for the present. That doesn't mean you can't look to the future, but you are marketing to people today. They need to be able to benefit from your innovation now.

MAINTAINING SUCCESS

Success is not a place you arrive at and can rest in. It is a practice that keeps you constantly striving for improvement.

Keeping Your Business on Track

Continuous Quality Improvement (CQI)

This term has been used frequently in the behavioral healthcare industry. The ideal of CQI is a business that regularly looks at its internal operations, and how these interface with the customer, and seeks constantly to improve all these processes. The use of outcomes measures services this process.

Total Quality Management (TQM)

When the total picture of the business is addressed, not just one department or only the inner operations, TQM is the operative word.

Inner Quality Management (IQM)

This term is not heard as frequently, but it is thought to be the foundation for both CQI and TQM. When there is a lack of inner or personal self-management, most people are not equipped to deal with the mental and emotional fluctuations they go through in relation to their work. These changes can have a profound impact on job performance and personal relationships. When people manage their inner life and feel that they have control over their future, they are better communicators, more cooperative and flexible and can deal with crises more effectively.

If you had someone tracking the stress-related reactions to the demands of business—the hormonal changes due to negative thinking about the unknown future—you would become a firm believer in IQM. By using IQM, fear can be channeled into creative action and future thinking reframed into positive uncertainty. When IQM is in place, and a CQI approach is used in business, the head and heart or inner business will work in tandem with the outer business. This sets the platform for longitudinal success.

Inner quality management is also called "championship living," "optimal performance," "self-management," and other terms coined by those in the field. It is usually based on a holistic model addressing the needs of the body, mind, emotions, and spirit. When I provide training for self-management, I also include relationships, work, and service to others.

Benefits of Inner Quality Management

- *Freedom.* You will find a great freedom realizing you are always true to your inner spirit. Your sense of personal freedom will allow you to enjoy each moment as it unfolds.
- *Momentum.* When your life is integrated and you are operating out of your personal life vision, you no longer need external motivation. Your inner drive toward perfection or entelechy moves you easily forward.
- *Integration.* When your life is integrated, each area works naturally to support all aspects of self. This creates a natural, organic foundation for growth.
- *Power.* There is great personal power in knowing you are being true to your self. No one can dissuade you or move you off your path, at least not for long.

How to Begin Inner Quality Management

Step 1

Begin by assessing the seven arenas of your life. On a scale from 1 to 5, 1 = needs work, 5 = looks good; ask yourself where you stand. The seven arenas are:

1. Body.
2. Mind.
3. Emotions.
4. Spirit.
5. Work.
6. Relationships.
7. Service to others or the community.

Step 2

If you rate an area as three or lower, you need to set some goals to bring it up to a four or five. Ask yourself what would improve the quality of this life arena. Avoid goals that are motivated outside or by others; these goals need to be yours. They also need to be SMART:

- Specific.
- Measurable.
- Accessible.
- Realistic.
- Timely.

When you set a goal, do a reality check or SMART check and ask yourself whether it fits these criteria.

Step 3

Now, break down each goal into manageable projects. You may have decided to increase your knowledge in a new specialty. This involves more than one task. You need to find out where to get the training, find the money to pay for it, find the time to do it. Each aspect of the goal needs a project and plan for accomplishment.

Step 4

When your plan is in place, it is time to schedule activities that will take you to your goals in small persistent steps. This is where the self-management comes into play. You need to become inner directed rather than outer directed. I keep a self-management organizer that has all my life projects in the front and a calendar in the back. This forces me to address my inner goals before I fill in someone else's plans for me in the calendar. The Professional Practice Review is a tool I created for consulting clients to help them manage themselves by constantly reevaluating the actions they are taking with their practice (see Figure 9.2).

Self-Management and Motivation

Managing yourself is very much like managing a business. There are fundamentals to observe. Enough has been discovered about human motivation in the past 25 years to show that attainment of inner satisfaction or *self-actualization,* as Abraham Maslow calls it, depends on authenticity. Internal motivation is connected to how intense your feelings are about achieving an objective. Achieving small passionate goals prepares you for achieving larger ones. For example, if you desire a trip to France as a long-term goal, go to French restaurants, learn the language, and take a course in French art or literature.

All individual needs begin with desire. What do you want more than anything else? Recognition, power, wealth, prestige? These needs can be satisfied in as many ways as there are people. People who love their work find it life-giving, natural, and enjoyable. Your work should be as natural as your play.

How well you manage yourself depends on your locus of control. The ideal—to manage yourself from the inside out—means that you assume responsibility for your actions and measure all external impacts on your time and energy against your internal values, purposes, and goals. For some, the locus of control works from the outside in; they are a slave to their calendar and the needs of other people and the environment. These people do not have a clear sense of personal purpose and lose a sense of who they are. To balance the two modes of management, you must keep an eye to the needs of the external world and your personal needs. As a human being, you have a responsibility to live in harmony with the planet and those who live here with you. Communication, negotiation, and caring for the needs of others while maintaining personal integrity compose the dance of life.

Just as executives use an individual management style to manage their company or subordinates, each of us has a personal management style, or mode of operating, that makes us most productive. When we work in a way that is consistent with our style, we get more done with less stress. Knowing about yourself provides you with the tools to work effectively with greater ease. Do you know the answers to the following questions:

Figure 9.2

Business Review

At the end of each week, ask yourself:

1. Which goals from last week did I meet?
2. What will I do about my unmet goals?
3. What are my goals for next week (e.g., phone calls, letters, presentations)?
4. How many referrals did I receive this week and what were the primary sources?
5. What did I do or not do to contribute to each cancellation and/or no-show?
6. Caseload Review—Go over case notes for each client and ask yourself:
    A. What can I do to facilitate growth?
    B. Do I need consultation on any client?
    C. Should any cases be terminated?
    D. Is the paperwork up to date?
7. Contacts: How could I improve my outreach? What colleagues do I want to see this week?
8. How much time did I donate to social services?
9. How have I grown professionally?
10. Are administrative details up to date?
11. Have I spent quality time with friends and family?
12. Have I taken care of my physical and mental fitness?

Is it still worth it?

- What are the times of the day or night you feel most productive?
- How do you organize your work before you begin?
- What motivates you to start working?
- What skills do you have and prefer to use?
- Would you prefer to have a regular schedule or work spontaneously?

Each person will find some questions easier to answer than others. These are the kinds of things you need to understand about yourself to manage yourself well. Two good self-management systems are the DayRunner®, available in most stationery stores and the Franklin System®, available from Franklin Company.

Balance

In all things, personal or professional balance is the key to continued success. When you communicate, you must balance good speaking skills with good listening skills. As a leader, you balance direction and control with following and discovery. The key to mastering your performance is having the ability to handle all sides of your life. Achieving balance requires flexibility as new situations call for different responses. Ideally, your life is dynamic; when you reach a balance, it will move to imbalance. It is your responsibility to know where you stand and make corrections back to center. The concept of *satori* is a means for life balancing. Satori refers to the natural harmony of body, mind, and emotions, defined as:

- Mind—pure attention.
- Emotions—motivational energy.
- Body—relaxed and vital sensitivity.

When all of these qualities are working in harmony, balance is the result. When you find one arena of your life, such as work, consuming most of your resources, it is time to rebalance your activities.

Getting Organized

Creative, active people are often the most disorganized. They may unconsciously recognize that disorganization, in its many forms, has payoffs that seem to outweigh the drawbacks.

Disorganization often invites the solicitude of friends and family. It's a good attention—and sympathy—invitation. Disorganization can also be used to gain reassurance that you are loved. The premise is if you wait for me that means you care. Many women, especially working mothers, also find it tough to take time for themselves. Being a bit disorganized can ensure a few moments away for it all during the day.

People often create disorganization to keep busy, so no one can accuse them, and they can't accuse themselves of not trying hard. Not trying hard has its payoffs, too. If you fail, you can always comfort yourself with the knowledge that you didn't really give it your best effort and could have succeeded if you had really tried.

Some conscious or unconscious fears of really getting on track could include:

- I don't want to be successful; just thinking of the responsibility scares me.
- No one in my family is successful and they will all get angry if I am.
- I can't be more successful than _________ or he (she) will not like/love me.
- I haven't figured out what successful is yet.
- What will I do after I am successful?

- It's lonely at the top.
- I'll have to make all new friends.
- I won't be able to afford it.
- Everybody else will be better than I am.
- I won't know how to act.
- I won't have time to spend with my family/cat.
- I don't have the wardrobe, car, teeth.
- I won't be able to be me any more.
- People will know who I am (and not like me).

Do any of these apply to you? It may be time to reframe success.

Why We Overload and When

Small disasters such as missed deadlines, lost keys, delayed or forgotten appointments, or an important file misplaced can eventually upset personal peace of mind and threaten professional success if they happen often enough.

Experts point to various psychological bases for disorganized behavior. One is *passive aggressive,* using disorganization to express anger instead of confronting a problem directly. If you don't want to do something, it is often easier to say "I don't have enough time" than to admit, "I don't want to do that for you."

Disorganization sometimes has its roots in childhood. Overly critical parents might only give their children attention when their bedroom is a mess or they don't get their homework in on time. The children say unconsciously, "This behavior works, I got their attention," and they grow up to be disorganized adults. They might also learn a sense of futility: "What's the point of finishing anything if nothing I do is good enough?"

Insecurity is another source of disorganization. People who take too long to do things usually fear not performing well. They overresearch and overwork because they're afraid of making mistakes, of missing something, of being found wanting. Then there are those who are obsessed with putting everything in its right place. Obsessive neatness is one way of dispelling anxiety and making you feel more in control, but it does not necessarily mean you are in control.

Conversely, someone whose home or office is messy may not necessarily be disorganized. It may be that they are organized in a way you do not recognize. I teach classes on personal organization and find that no two people ever organize information in the same way. Finally, a surprisingly common contributor to disorganization is an underlying fear of death. It's not at all uncommon for people to hold an almost magical belief that if they haven't met all their responsibilities, nothing can happen to them, they can't be taken away yet. There's comfort in keeping things undone.

Letting Go of Chaos

It's important to realize that a little chaos does not mean you lack intelligence or are a bad person. To maintain self-esteem, people develop many defenses against disorganization, especially denial and guilt. For example, a young woman signaled to make a left-hand turn, and turned to the right. Her companion pointed out the discrepancy, and she snapped "That's what I meant" as if the friend had been at fault for not reading her mind. Guilt, on the other hand, haunts owners of messy offices and living rooms, which keeps them from ever making a change. One way to overcome this obstacle is to close the door, pretend the room belongs to someone who has just moved out and you are going in to clean up and organize. This provides a fresh perspective and freedom from the belief that it's all your fault.

Remember, chaos and clarity are necessary conditions for all creative acts and no one has every aspect of his or her life under control. Trying to live up to an unattainable ideal can make your life miserable.

Organizing to Free Creativity

How successful you will be at changing your habits has to do with motivation. The ideal motivation is the desire to go after what you really want in life instead of settling for what you get. Although many fear that organization inhibits creativity, that's really a misconception. In truth, organization frees you for creative activity. Once you have a basic understanding of how you function and identify your personal priorities, the process becomes simple because you will organize your life to meet the needs of your inner self.

The Happy Healer

Many years ago, I created a course called the Happy Healer. My intention was to provide tools to help mental health professionals remain healthy and able to practice their craft for many years. I was motivated to create this course after working many years in psychiatric hospitals and watching the toll the system took on my staff. The work was difficult; the staffing was always short; people were asked to work double shifts; supplies and resources were difficult to obtain; and staff weren't recognized for their hard work, only their mistakes.

It became clear these mental health professionals needed to take responsibility for their own wellness, and this is still the case in private practice. Individual practitioners infrequently receive praise for their work, and if it comes from a client, they can't tell others. Because their referral bases are vulnerable to others, they often work long hours to make the money they need or to accommodate clients' needs. Some of the tools I recommend for professionals are:

- Supervision.
- A personal journal.
- Planned vacations.
- Diversification in their work.
- Constantly keeping an eye on boundaries, making time for self-renewal.
- Maintaining a professional support system through individuals and groups.
- Networking with other professionals.
- Taking personal retreats to review their work and where it is going.

When helping others is hurting you, there is a problem. If this is the case in your life, get help now. Do what you often wish your clients would do; don't wait for the bottom to fall out.

Conclusion

My goal in writing this book is to motivate and provide tools for mental health professionals so they can create fulfilling practices for themselves and become a resource for their communities. The mental health profession is changing rapidly, and we can either react or become proactive in cocreating our futures. I invite you to take control of your professional future and to work with others in redefining the role of the mental health professional as individual healer, family resource, and advocate for healthy social change. If you wait for others to define your future, you will be disappointed. Together we can succeed.

BIBLIOGRAPHY

American Psychiatric Association. (1994). *Diagnostic and statistical manual of mental disorders* (4th ed.). Washington, DC: Author.

Boldt, L. (1993). *Zen and the art of making a living—A practical guide to creative career design.* New York: Penguin.

Clark. (1993). *Networking.* Mission, KS: Skillpath Publications

Clifford, D., & Warner, R. (1993). *The partnership book: How to write a partnership agreement* (4th ed.). Berkeley, CA: Nolo Press.

Covey, S.R. (1989). *The 7 habits of highly effective people—Powerful lessons in personal change.* New York: Simon & Schuster.

Directory of Experts, Authorities and Spokespersons. (1995). Washington, DC: Broadcast Interview Source.

Drucker, P.F. (1985). *Innovation and entrepreneurship: Practice and principles.* New York: Harper & Row.

Garvey, M. (Ed.). (1993). *1994 writer's market: Where and how to sell what you write.* Cinncinati, OH: Writers Digest Books.

Gold, M. (1994). *The foundations of your private practice* (Vols. 1–2). Alameda, CA: Hunter House.

Gropp, M.M. (1982). *VALS—As a media evaluation tool.* New York: Magazine Publishers Association.

Horton, W., Taylor, L., Ignacio, A., & Hoft, N.L. (1996). The web page design cookbook. New York: John Wiley & Sons.

Huang, C.A., & Lynch, J. (1992). *Thinking body, dancing mind—Tao sports for extraordinary performance in athletics, business, and life.* New York: Bantam.

Jenkins, D.J., & Curtis, J.F. (1985). *Starting and operating a business in Massachusetts.* Grants Pass, OR: Oasis Press.

Kubler-Ross, E. (1993). *On death and dying.* New York: Collier Books.

Lant, J.L. (1981). *The consultant's kit—Establishing and operating your successful consulting business.* Cambridge, MA: JLA.

Martin, I. (1996). *From couch to corporation.* New York: John Wiley & Sons.

Maslow, A.H. (1972). *The farther reaches of human nature.* New York: Penguin Books.

Ornish, D. (1990). *Dr. Dean Ornish's program for reversing heart disease.* New York: Random House.

Oss, M.E., & McBride, D.L. (1996). Finding best practices guidelines. *Open Minds, 10*(2), 8–9.

Prochaska, J., & DiClemente, C. (1982). Transtheoretical therapy: Toward a more integrative model of change. *Psychotherapy: Theory, Research, and Practice, 19*(3), 276–288.

Prochaska, J.O., Norcross, J.C., & DiClemente, C. (1994). *Changing for good: The revolutionary program that explains the six stages of change and teaches you how to free yourself from bad habits.* New York: William Morrow.

Putman, A.O. (1990). *Marketing your services.* New York: John Wiley & Sons.

Ray, P.H. (1996, Spring). The rise of integral culture. *Noetic Sciences Review,* 4–15.

Rosen, M. (1997). *The mental health technology bible.* New York: John Wiley & Sons.

Senge, P. (1994). *The fifth discipline fieldbook.* New York: Dell.

Shenson, H.L. (1990). *The contract and fee-setting guide for consultants & professionals.* New York: John Wiley & Sons.

Skovholt, T.M., & Ronnestad, M.H. (1992). *The evolving professional self: Stages and themes in therapist and counselor development.* New York: John Wiley & Sons.

Zuckerman, E. (1991). *The clinician's thesaurus—A guidebook for wording psychological reports and other evaluations* (2nd ed.). Pittsburgh, PA: The Three Wishes Press.

Zuckerman, E., & Guyett, I.P.R. (1991). *The paper office—The tools to make your small psychotherapy practice work ethically, legally and profitably: Forms, guidelines, and resources.* Pittsburgh, PA: The Three Wishes Press.

INDEX

INDEX

INDEX